Grocery List:

✓ cocoa powder

brown sugar

✓ salted butter

eggs

honey

~~chocolate chips~~

heavy whipping cream

From the Kitchen of

Sookie St. James

Sookie's Recipe Book

An Official Cookbook

Recipes Inspired by Stars Hollow and the Independence and Dragonfly Inns

By Sookie St. James

INSIGHT EDITIONS

SAN RAFAEL · LOS ANGELES · LONDON

Contents

Chapter Four: Sandwiches, Salads & Sides

Chapter Five: Mains

Chapter Six: Drinks, Cocktails & Mixes

Chapter Seven: Desserts

Introduction

Norman Mailer (may you rest in peace), I wrote a cookbook!

Welcome to my cookbook! Norman Mailer, someone is perusing my cookbook right now! If you could see me now!

It took a little longer than I planned, 'cause I had to wait for the bleeding to die down. (Those eureka moments hit a little different when you're in a hot kitchen with knives and flames and oil all over the floor. You gotta watch out for those . . . lunging . . . chops . . . . But it's fine, I'm fine, everything's totally fine! Only three stitches!)

Fine? What? Sookie St. James is thriving. I'm spectacular. I'm fantastic. I'm spectastic. I married the cutest produce vendor slash food engineer god on this side of the international dateline, and we have three gorgeous kids. (For the record, they all love jalapeño in their mac and cheese, too. Because that's how we do it in the Hollow.)

Every day I go to the inn (the Dragonfly Inn, for the uninitiated) I co-own and run with my very best friend, Lorelai Gilmore, cook the food I love to cook, and experiment with new flavor profiles and ingredients (and sometimes weird franken-foods no one asked for, okay), all in service of making the most beloved dishes for my most beloved people.

It's simple, but to me food is love. (You can sing the Dean song—I know you want to.) I'm not always so quick with the perfect quip or comeback, and I know as well as anyone how easy it is to misunderstand when BIG FEELINGS are on the line. As Lorelai once said, "When your heart's involved, it all comes out in moron," and even the best of us have gotten stuck at "hi" on a first date.

This being Stars Hollow, you never know what you might see or hear. (Kirk's butt, all stuck with thorns? But that probably won't happen to you.) People are weird and complicated. Relationships take unexpected twists. When you're having trouble connecting, sometimes it's as simple as a cup of pudding, or a picnic basket, or a rocky road cookie for your new crush, to send a signal: I see you. I'm here. I'm listening.

It all comes back to the food. It's my responsibility as your local charmingly eccentric co-innkeeper/chef to be sure you try new and exciting foods even when you don't want to. Whether it's a wake for a cat or a Sweet 16 party, a bake sale buffet, or an impromptu family dinner . . . food brings us together in a basic and undeniable way. And I'm just so, so happy it's brought you here!

Now if you'll excuse me, I think one of my stitches opened, so I'm just going to go take care of the bleeding.

Bon Appétit!

xoxo,
Sookie

pineapple infused vodka
vodka
bacon infused vodka
ginger syrup
brandied cherries

Chapter One: The Pantry

Yield: 2 loaves
V

SPECIAL TOOLS:

- Two 9- by 5-inch loaf pans
- Kitchen thermometer

- ¼ cup plus 1 tablespoon water, divided
- 5½ tablespoons granulated sugar, divided
- 2 tablespoons whole milk
- 3½ teaspoons (about 1½ packets) active dry yeast
- 4½ cups all-purpose flour, plus more for the work surface
- 1½ teaspoons salt
- 6 eggs (1 egg separated), divided
- 1 cup (16 tablespoons) unsalted butter, preferably European style, at room temperature but cool (see note), plus more for greasing the pans
- Vegetable oil, for greasing the bowl

NOTE: The butter should be at room temperature but still cool to the touch. You should be able to make a shallow imprint in it by pressing it with your finger, but it should not be melty or squishy.

Homemade Brioche Bread

What smells more delicious than fresh-baked bread? Maybe freshly baking bread, but that's a real humdinger of a hairsplitter. At the Independence Inn, we always kept a variety of loaves on the counter every day. So I'm sure it comes as no surprise that the tradition lives on at our beloved Dragonfly. Most mornings, Dragonfly guests are greeted by the rich, eggy-sweet scent of my—if I do say so myself—unparalleled, light-as-a-feather brioche bread. Pillow-soft, puffy, and buttery—and so easy to make (but still plenty impressive). This one's perfect for sweet, airy weekend brunch French toast (see the Caramelized Hazelnut Brioche French Toast recipe on page 47).

Buttery brioche bliss. Blammo. You're welcome.

In a heatproof measuring cup or small bowl, combine ¼ cup of the water, 1 tablespoon of the sugar, and the milk. Heat to very warm, between 100°F and 110°F. Sprinkle the yeast over the mixture, stir to combine, and set aside until foamy, about 5 minutes.

In the bowl of a stand mixer fitted with a dough hook or a large mixing bowl if using a hand mixer, add the remaining 4½ tablespoons of sugar, the flour, and the salt and stir to combine. Add the yeast mixture, and with the mixer on low, add five eggs plus one yolk, one at a time. Refrigerate the remaining egg white in an airtight container; this will be for your egg wash. Continue mixing on low until a soft dough begins to form, about 5 minutes.

Cut the butter into tablespoon-size pieces. With the mixer on low, add 2 tablespoons at a time, and wait until those pieces are completely incorporated before adding more. Stop the mixer and scrape down the dough hook and bowl as needed. It will take between 15 and 20 minutes to add all the butter. Once all the butter is added, knead the dough for another 7 to 10 minutes or until it starts to form a ball. The dough will still be quite sticky but it should be easy to coax it away from the sides and bottom of the bowl.

Grease a large bowl lightly with the vegetable oil and put the dough in it. Cover it tightly with plastic wrap and refrigerate it overnight (at least 8 hours or up to 24).

buttery
brioche
bliss

Butter the loaf pans. To shape the dough, lightly flour a work surface. Turn the dough out onto the surface and use a bench scraper or knife to cut it in half. Work with one half at a time, keeping the second one covered in the bowl. Cut the first half of the dough into thirds. Roll each third out into a rope about 15 inches long. Pinch three ends together, do a basic braid, and pinch the bottom ends together. Place the braid in one of the greased loaf pans, tucking the ends under, and cover it tightly with plastic wrap. Repeat with the second half of the dough.

Allow to proof in a warm place or an oven with a proofing setting until the dough reaches the top of the pan. This can take 1½ to 2½ hours depending on the warmth of the environment. The ideal temperature is between 74°F and 80°F and draft-free.

Toward the end of the proof, preheat the oven to 400°F. When the bread is ready to bake, mix the remaining egg white with the remaining 1 tablespoon of water, whisk, and brush over the top of each loaf. Bake for 10 minutes and then lower the oven to 350°F and bake for another 20 to 25 minutes. Once the crust is a golden brown, cover with foil and continue to bake until the bread sounds hollow when tapped on top or the internal temperature reaches 190°F.

Remove the bread from the pans immediately and cool on a wire rack. Serve with butter and jam, use to make sandwiches, or use to make Caramelized Hazelnut Brioche French Toast (page 47).

Store in a plastic bag or airtight container for up to 5 days.

"Bid on a Basket" Pineapple-Cranberry Chutney

Oh, chutney. I love chutney. It's such a fun word to say—try it! Chutney.

This recipe's extra near and dear to me, because I developed it for Jackson's Stars Hollow auction basket the year we got engaged. (Mind you, the whole thing was almost a disaster—the man barged into the kitchen like some kind of . . . crazed barger while I was baking and came this close to ruining everything. The contents of the baskets are supposed to be a surprise.)

"Oh sure, never see a pie before an auction," Jackson said (quite sarcastically) at the time. (This was right after the barging.) "Everyone knows that expression."

Well, I don't care if it's not an expression—it should be! I ended up missing Jackson's hints about moving in together, so he let Kirk bid on my beautiful basket with this cozy, gingery, just-for-Jackson pineapple-cranberry chutney. The whole day was a complete disaster! Until he proposed at the end of it. That also happened that day; it's probably worth mentioning.

Yield: About 3 cups
V, V+, GF

SPECIAL TOOL:

- Three 8-ounce jars, sterilized (see tip)

- 2 tablespoons light olive oil
- 1 medium yellow onion, finely chopped
- 3 cloves garlic, finely chopped
- 1 tablespoon finely chopped ginger (about 1-inch piece fresh ginger)
- 4 cardamom pods
- 2 star anise pods
- 2 cinnamon sticks, broken into pieces
- ½ cup packed light or dark brown sugar
- ⅓ cup cider vinegar
- 3 cups chopped fresh pineapple, cut into small chunks (about ½ pineapple)
- ½ cup dried cranberries
- ½ teaspoon salt
- ⅛ to ¼ teaspoon red pepper flakes

In a large saucepan over medium heat, heat the oil. Add the onion, garlic, ginger, cardamom, star anise, and cinnamon sticks. Cook for 5 minutes until fragrant. Lower the heat to medium-low and cook for 20 minutes, stirring occasionally, or until the onions are very soft. Add the brown sugar, vinegar, pineapple, cranberries, salt, and red pepper flakes. Simmer, covered, over medium-low heat for 20 minutes, stirring occasionally. Uncover and cook for another 30 to 40 minutes until it becomes dark golden and thick. Remove the star anise and cinnamon at this stage or allow them to continue to flavor the chutney in the jars. Pour into sterilized jars (see tip). Cool to room temperature and cover with a tight lid. Refrigerate overnight or for up to 3 weeks.

TIP: To easily sterilize your jars, wash well with soap, rinse well, and arrange them standing up without touching on a rimmed baking sheet. Put the tray into a preheated 350°F oven for 10 minutes. Meanwhile, bring a medium saucepan filled halfway with water to a boil over high heat. Add the lids and boil for 10 minutes. Use this time to make the chutney. Remove the lids from the water using tongs and place on a clean dish towel to dry.

Famous Peach Sauce

Yield: 2 cups
V, V+, GF

SPECIAL TOOL:

- Immersion blender

- 3 or 4 fresh peaches, peeled, pitted, and sliced
- 3 tablespoons maple syrup
- 1 tablespoon packed dark brown sugar
- Juice from 1 lemon (about 2 tablespoons)
- ¼ cup water
- ½ teaspoon vanilla paste

It's the obvious pun, I know, but this sauce is truly peachy keen. Which I think you'll agree is something one wants from a peach sauce. Maybe the main thing?

And you can keep your Georgia peaches, which like to steal all the regional-fruit thunder (that absolutely is a real thing)—I'll stick with Jackson's Connecticut grown, thank you very much.

Now, did I spend days . . . weeks . . . okay, months . . . perfecting this one? Making sure the ratio of just-tapped maple syrup and peach reduction was in total harmony? Oh, the exact total amount of time isn't important (though Lorelai could probably give you a close estimate)—let's just say it was an investment. But I challenge any chef out there to tell me it wasn't worthwhile. This sauce would never strangle that perfect summer-peach flavor—it lets them sing! (But not literally, like Jackson does to his persimmons when they've been coming in sour.)

I first created this sauce for waffles on the Independence brunch menu, but it's super versatile. Try it with the brioche (page 10)! Or mix it into milkshakes, or pour over pound cake, or, or, or . . . !

In a medium saucepan over low heat, combine the peaches, maple syrup, brown sugar, lemon juice, and water. Warm the mixture slowly until the sugar has dissolved, stirring gently, for 2 to 3 minutes.

Increase the temperature to medium-high and continue cooking the mixture until the fruit is very tender and begins to break apart, 10 to 15 minutes.

Remove from the heat and use an immersion blender to purée the mixture until very smooth. Return to the stove over medium heat, add the vanilla paste, and bring to a gentle simmer. Cook for 2 to 3 minutes until warmed through.

Serve immediately with Belgian Waffles (page 34) or Homemade Brioche Bread (page 10) and butter.

To store, allow to cool to room temperature and refrigerate in an airtight container for up to 4 days or freeze for up to 1 month.

TIP: If fresh peaches aren't in season or your farmer brings you "watery" ones, use 16 ounces of frozen peaches instead.

Brandied Cherries

Yield: 2 cups
V, V+, GF

SPECIAL TOOL:

- One 16-ounce or two 8-ounce jars, sterilized (see tip page 13)

- ½ cup cherry juice or water (see note)
- ⅔ cup granulated sugar
- 1 cup brandy
- 1 pound fresh cherries, pitted, or 2 cups frozen or jarred cherries (see note)

Another happy accident, this pantry staple evolved from a cherry compote I developed when Emily Gilmore tapped us to cater a launch party for Richard's new business venture with Jason "Digger" Stiles. (No, I still don't know why his nickname was, is, and seems to remain Digger. I try not to judge.)

The "us" in this case being, of course, Lorelai and me. Which initially threw Lorelai for a loop because she hadn't mentioned to Emily that there was an "us" with a catering business in the first place, so she was sure her mother would be furious to find out from me. (And that was one of the less intense reasons Lorelai thought taking the gig would be a bad idea.)

I managed to talk her into it by reminding her of the wads of pretty, pretty money we'd get to take home, and before you knew it, we were soaking fresh cherries in a patented brandy syrup (and, apparently, "tarting up" Rory's bedroom in the process).

Did it turn out that Digger put the kibosh on the launch party as too fussy and traditional? Was all that hard work and quiche-ing up of home interiors ultimately a waste of time? No, because we have brandied cherries to show for it. Now life can be your very own ice-cream sundae. Cherries on top.

In a medium saucepan over medium heat, combine the cherry juice and sugar. Bring to a low simmer, stirring, and cook until the sugar has dissolved, about 5 minutes. Increase the heat to medium-high and bring to a boil for 2 minutes. Add the brandy and cherries, stirring until well coated.

Put the cherries into a sterilized 2-cup jar, or two sterilized 1-cup jars (see tip page 13), adding enough liquid to cover. Allow to cool to room temperature before sealing with a lid. Refrigerate at least overnight, but preferably 1 week (or up to 3 months) before serving.

NOTE: Thaw frozen cherries over a strainer into a jar and use the released liquid as part of the juice or water. Alternatively, drain the liquid from jarred Morello cherries, retaining the liquid to use according to the recipe.

Apple Chutney

Another chutney, in case you doubted my love of both the word and the condiment. Also another chance for you to try saying it out loud again, if you were too busy being very serious and too cool for school for those kinds of things the first time around:

CHUT. NEY. Yay!

This one is warm and wintry with notes of ginger, currants, and apple cider vinegar. The tangy blend complements a perfectly roasted pork tenderloin as well as elevating your standard comfort-food grilled cheese sandwich. I used Jackson's apples (of course) to make this for the sweet potato biscuits we served at Chin-Chin's memorial service.

Come to think of it, we spend a decent amount of time cooking for pet funerals here in Stars Hollow. And it's not even the tip of the iceberg re: the quirkiest thing we do. Hay bale mazes, knitathons, festivals of the living arts . . . And some of us also really like running around yelling "chutney" at the top of our lungs.

I think that is just you. —Michel

Yield: About 2 cups
V, V+, GF

SPECIAL TOOL:

- Two 8-ounce jars or one 16-ounce jar, sterilized (see tip page 13)

- 2 tablespoons light olive oil
- 1 cup finely chopped Vidalia or yellow onion
- 3 cloves garlic, finely chopped
- 1 tablespoon finely chopped ginger (about 1-inch piece fresh ginger)
- 4 cardamom pods
- 8 whole cloves
- 2 star anise pods
- 2 cinnamon sticks, broken into pieces
- ½ cup packed light brown sugar
- ⅓ cup cider vinegar
- 3 cups peeled (about 2 large) green apples, cut into ⅓-inch cubes
- ⅓ cup raisins
- ½ teaspoon salt

In a medium saucepan over medium heat, heat the oil. Add the onion, garlic, ginger, cardamom, cloves, star anise, and cinnamon sticks. Cook for 5 minutes until fragrant. Lower the heat to low and cook for 20 minutes, stirring often, or until the onions are very soft. Add the brown sugar, vinegar, apples, raisins, and salt. Cover the pan and simmer over medium-low heat for 20 minutes, stirring occasionally. Uncover and simmer for another 10 to 15 minutes, stirring often, until almost all the liquid evaporates. Remove the star anise and cinnamon at this stage or allow them to continue to flavor the chutney in the jars. Transfer to sterilized jars (see tip page 13). Cool to room temperature and cover with a tight lid. Serve the same day or refrigerate for up to 4 weeks.

Yes, it was a lovely memorial we put on for your dog, Michel. You're welcome. —Lorelai

Infused Vinegars & Olive Oils

Blackberry-Rosemary Vinegar

Yield: 1 cup vinegar; about 1½ cups pickled blackberries
V, V+, GF

SPECIAL TOOL:

- One 16-ounce or two 8-ounce jars, sterilized (see tip page 13)

- 2 cups fresh blackberries (about 12 ounces)
- ¾ cup white wine or red wine vinegar
- 1 cup granulated sugar
- 4 small sprigs rosemary

Did I mention I have the most amazing produce supplier? He's so fantastic that, dear reader, I married him! So that's the bad news—Jackson Belleville is a taken man. But that doesn't mean you can't sample his blackberries sometime. (I hope that doesn't sound dirty?!)

Yep—hold on to your taste buds, because if you've never tried one of Jackson's early summer blackberries, there's good news aplenty on the way. (And for once, the good news is not that I won't be able to make the strawberry shortcake! Although if it were, I'd just make it with blackberries!) Blackberry boom? No problem! I pickle them for year-round use.

It's all about the blackberries, people—and this recipe captures them at their peak summer sweet-tart perfection. Steep the fruit and the herbs in the vinegar for a week-ish—you gotta watch 'em like sleeping babies, but 10 days is usually my max—before straining. Then you can store in the fridge to enjoy all season long. This is a great flavor boost for all kinds of salads—especially my own signature Watermelon, Peach, and Feta with Mint Salad (page 85), a staple at the Dragonfly.

Gently wash and dry the blackberries.

In a medium saucepan over medium heat, combine the vinegar and sugar. Bring to a low simmer, stirring, and cook until the sugar has dissolved, about 5 minutes. Increase the heat to medium-high and bring to a boil. Boil gently for 2 minutes. Put the blackberries into a sterilized 2-cup jar or two sterilized 1-cup jars (see tip page 13), adding enough liquid to cover the blackberries. Allow to cool to room temperature and top with the rosemary sprigs before sealing with a lid. Refrigerate and steep for 7 to 10 days before straining. Use pickled blackberries in salads and as a garnish for cheese platters. Refrigerate the vinegar in a jar or bottle for up to 3 months.

Infused Vinegars & Olive Oils

Meyer Lemon-Infused Vinegar

Lorelai says she could tell Jackson and I were meant to be from the very first time she caught us bickering over a crate of blueberries. Somehow it's not the wackiest statement she's ever made. I kind of knew, too!

Jackson started as our produce guy who loved (still does) to find tiny ways to get under my skin—like suggesting I use his bumper crop of blueberries in place of strawberries in a traditional shortcake recipe. (Haha, okay, good one, Jackson.)

One thing we're in complete lockstep about is his totally divine Meyer lemon crop this season. So perfectly tart, just a squeeze will brighten any dish. It's the precise acidic balance for your favorite velvety-smooth EVOO, taking salads, sauces, and marinades to the next level.

Yield: 2 cups
V, GF

SPECIAL TOOL:

- One 16-ounce jar or bottle, sterilized (see tip page 13)

- 2 cups white wine, rice, or apple cider vinegar
- 3 Meyer lemons, sliced
- 2 sprigs thyme
- ¼ cup honey

Didion back from Jess? —Rory

Pour the vinegar into a medium saucepan. Holding each lemon slice over the saucepan to catch the juice, remove any visible seeds. Add the lemons and thyme to the vinegar. Over medium heat, simmer for 5 minutes. Using a slotted spoon, transfer the lemons to a 1-quart or two 16-ounce jars. Pour the liquid over the lemons and cover loosely. Once cool, tighten the lid and place in a cool spot for at least 7 days, or up to 3 weeks, shaking the jar once every day or two.

Strain into a small saucepan, pressing on the fruit to release as much juice as possible. Over medium-low heat, bring to a gentle simmer and add the honey. Stir until the honey has completely melted into the vinegar. Remove from the heat and allow to cool. Transfer to a sterilized jar or bottle (see tip page 13) and refrigerate for up to 3 months.

TIP: Once you have strained the fruit to make your finished vinegar, candy the already-softened rinds for another treat. Cut each slice into quarters, remove the flesh from the rind, and put into a small saucepan. Add ½ cup of water and 1 cup of sugar and bring to a boil over medium-high heat, stirring until the sugar has dissolved. Reduce the heat to medium-low and simmer for 1 hour, stirring occasionally. Strain the candied rind over a measuring cup or small bowl, reserving the syrup for sweetening Four Years without a Cocktail Mockaritas (page 126) or iced tea. Put the rind on a baking sheet lined with parchment paper, without letting them touch, to dry for 1 to 2 days, or in a dehydrator for about 4 hours at 135°F. Once they are only still slightly tacky, put 3 tablespoons of sugar in a soup bowl. Add the rind a few at a time and coat each piece with sugar before transferring to a plate or storage container. Store in an airtight container for up to 1 month at room temperature or put in a resealable bag and freeze for up to 6 months.

Renew Ottessa Moshfegh!
—Rory

Infused Vinegars & Olive Oils

Spice-Infused Olive Oils

I don't think I'm overstating it when I say that olive oil is basically a miracle elixir. In ancient times, it was used as fuel in lamps. Today, some folks recommend taking a teaspoon a day to stay heart-healthy. Personally, I'll stick to cooking with it, especially when it's one of my special spice-infused blends. A perfect, versatile base for dressings, sauces, and marinades (or, hey—how about olive the above, please? Ha!).

Yield: ½ cup per flavor
V, V+, GF

SPECIAL TOOL:

- One 6-ounce jar, sterlized (see tip page 13)

- 1 teaspoon whole coriander, pink peppercorn, or 2 or 3 chile peppers
- ½ cup olive oil (see note)

Put your choice of spice into the jar. Put the jar on a baking sheet, place in the cold oven, and heat the oven to 250°F. Once the oven reaches temperature, set a timer for 5 minutes.

Remove the tray from the oven and add the oil to the jar. Allow to cool to room temperature, then seal and store out of direct sunlight for up to 1 week. After 24 hours, taste the oil (this is especially important with the chile peppers)—if you don't want the flavor any stronger, strain into a bowl, discard the solids, and return the liquid to the jar.

NOTE: These olive oils should be consumed within 1 week, so only make what you can use up. I suggest making only one or two of the flavors at a time.

Yield: 2 cups
V, V+, GF

- 2 cups radishes (see note)
- 2 cups vinegar
- 1 cup water
- ¼ cup granulated sugar
- 1 tablespoon kosher salt
- ½ teaspoon black or white peppercorns

Pickled Radish Roses

When the day comes that we're ready to offer cooking lessons and other workshops at the Dragonfly, pickling is high on my list. It's a fun, creative way to be sure you get your veggies in, and you might be surprised at how wacky and innovative you can get with what you decide to brine.

Oh sure, anyone can slap a pickled cucumber on a pastrami sandwich—and why wouldn't you?! I've been known to duck behind the counter at Luke's during a lunch rush myself to do just that (not that Mr. Grumpypants appreciated the effort). But dream big, dreamer! How about a pickled radish rose? Or—what if?—pickled asparagus, anyone? Cauliflower! Green beans! A zucchini from Jackson's magical patch? (He sleeps with them, you know. That's not a euphemism.)

Pickled veggies are great in salads, in sandwiches, as a garnish, or right next to your standard baby carrots and hummus at a casual gathering. Look at you being all fancy with your pickled veggies!

This base for preserving veggies is quick and versatile. Stock up on mason jars and then buckle up for your new hobby slash obsession. For once, you'll be thrilled to the dills (sorry) to find yourself in a pickle, I promise.

Wash your radishes well. If you want to make them into roses, cut the tops and root bottoms off. From the top down, slice the first cut three-quarters of the way down, being careful not to slice all the way through. Rotate the radish and slice again, cutting halfway through the first slice, again three-quarters of the way down. Continue three more times. Alternatively, slice the radishes.

In a medium saucepan, combine the vinegar, water, sugar, salt, and peppercorns. Cook over medium heat, stirring, until the sugar dissolves, about 5 minutes. Divide the vegetables between one 20-ounce or two 12-ounce jars. Pour the vinegar mixture over the vegetables until completely covered. Allow to cool to room temperature before covering tightly with a lid. Refrigerate overnight or up to 1 month.

NOTE: Use this method to pickle other vegetables like sliced cucumbers, green beans, sliced red onions, or cauliflower florets.

Thank-You Jam

Yield: About 6 cups
V, GF

Nothing says "I appreciate you!" like a jar of fresh homemade jam. It's a great way to thank someone for doing you an enormous favor, like giving your deadbeat pal a job. (Assuming that person likes jam.) But how could they not love this one? A blend of Jackson's peaches and raspberries with a touch of spice, this spread sure ain't meant for your mother's peanut butter and jelly sandwich. (Unless your mother had an incredibly sophisticated palate.)

Anyway, that's why Jackson gifted this jam to Lorelai after she hired his cousin Rune to work at the Independence Inn. She loved it and used it on everything in our kitchen from scones to muffins to a sleeve of crackers I found hidden in her coat pocket one day. (Words were exchanged. Lorelai's palate is more like "high-low.")

Jam for all! Please and thank you!

HIGH-LOW? MORE LIKE LOW-LOW. —LUKE

Unnecessary. And PS: Rune did not work out. So, who's grateful for my trash palate now? —Lorelai

SPECIAL TOOLS:

- Six to eight 8-ounce jars, sterilized (see tip page 13)

- 3 cups peeled, chopped peaches
- 2 cups raspberries
- 6½ cups granulated sugar
- ⅓ cup lemon juice
- 1 tablespoon salted butter (optional)
- One 3-ounce package liquid pectin

In a large nonreactive pot over medium-high heat, combine the peaches, raspberries, sugar, and lemon juice. Stir until the sugar is dissolved, crushing the fruit a bit as you go. Add the butter, if using, and let the mixture come to a rolling boil (one that does not stop when stirred).

Add the pectin, bring back to a boil, and cook for 1 minute. Remove from the heat and ladle into the jars, leaving ¼ inch of headspace. Seal and refrigerate or can using your favorite method.

Yield: 8 cups
(10 to 12 servings)
V+*, GF*

- 1 bulb garlic plus 6 to 8 cloves, divided
- ¼ cup plus 1 teaspoon olive oil, divided
- 3 to 5 anchovy fillets, from a tin packed in oil
- 3 tablespoons capers
- Two 28-ounce cans crushed tomatoes
- 1 cup kalamata olives, pitted
- ¼ cup balsamic vinegar or your favorite red wine
- Freshly ground black pepper
- 1 cup fresh basil leaves, for serving
- Shaved Parmesan, for serving (optional)

NOTE: To make this sauce vegan, replace the anchovy with 1 tablespoon of white miso and serve with vegan pasta and a Parmesan substitute. To make gluten free, serve with gluten-free pasta.

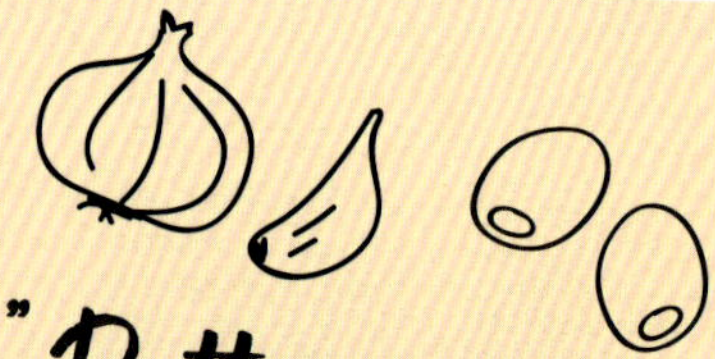

Tomato Sauce: "Godfather It Up" Puttanesca

You know what never took off in Stars Hollow? The low-carb diet trend. Is there anything more satisfying than a heaping bowl of fresh-made pasta on a crisp autumn evening? (Maybe a snowy winter evening. I bet that's what Lorelai would say.) But you do you—there's no wrong way to carb in Stars Hollow. Unless you skimp out on the sauce.

This tomato sauce is a traditional puttanesca, loaded with garlic, capers, olives, and anchovies. It's bold, fragrant, and sure to pull you out of any food funk. Make this ahead in batches for freezing and break it out at the first signs of the first winter frost . . . Or whip up a fresh pot any time you want your house to smell like Antonioli's kitchen. Go big, like giant pizza big! Godfather it up, and for sure feel free to measure that garlic with your heart. Puttanesca is meant to pack a (non-mobster-stereotype, nonliteral) punch.

Preheat the oven to 375°F.

Cut off the top of the garlic bulb, exposing some of the cloves, and drizzle with 1 teaspoon of the oil. Wrap it in foil and put in a baking dish. Bake for 25 to 30 minutes or until the cloves are fork-tender. Set aside to cool. When cool enough to handle, squeeze the cloves out of their skins.

Place the anchovy fillets into a small bowl, mince the remaining garlic cloves, and add them to the anchovy. Use a fork to combine, gently breaking up the anchovy fillets.

In a large sauté pan over medium heat, add the remaining ¼ cup of oil, heat for 1 minute, and then add the anchovy mixture. Sauté, stirring frequently, for 3 to 5 minutes or until the anchovy is mostly dissolved.

Add the capers and the crushed tomatoes, stir to combine, and cook until it just begins to bubble, 3 to 5 minutes. Turn the heat down to medium-low and add the olives. Continue to stir frequently so that the sauce does not bubble too much, about 10 minutes. Add the balsamic vinegar and roasted garlic cloves, stir, and cook for another 10 to 15 minutes. Add the black pepper to taste.

At this point, the sauce can continue to stay warm on the stove while you prepare your favorite pasta or be left to cool for storage.

To serve, chiffonade the basil and toss it with the sauce and cooked pasta. Serve with shaved Parmesan, if desired.

No low-carb
trends
here!

Yield: 30 ounces
V

- 2 cups all-purpose flour, plus more for the work surface and as needed
- ¼ teaspoon kosher salt
- ½ teaspoon baking powder
- 2 cups plus 6 tablespoons (38 tablespoons total) cold unsalted butter, preferably European style, divided
- ½ cup sour cream

Quick Puff Pastry

Speaking of carbs . . . (I mean, anyone around here not named Michel is always up for carb talk . . .)

Here's another staple that you'll reach for again and again. This one is a from-scratch puff pastry recipe that can form the base for anything from Bracebridge Dinner Peacock Pie (page 111) to apple turnovers. Wrap them around tiny sausages for pigs in a blanket or fill them with chocolate for—yep, you guessed it—pain au chocolat. Get yourself one of those cake domy thingees or a gorgeous bread box you can see through because you'll be a bonafide pastry chef before you know it.

Just don't name any of your desserts until you're 100 percent sure they're keepers. You don't want to get attached. (You were a great cake, Clyde. Le sigh.)

In the bowl of a food processor, pulse the flour, salt, and baking powder two or three times to combine.

Cut 2 cups of the butter into tablespoon-size pieces and put the remaining 6 tablespoons in the freezer. Add the cut-up butter to the food processor. Pulse on and off until the butter has been broken down into large pea-size pieces. Add the sour cream and pulse until the dough just starts to hold together.

Turn the dough out into a lightly floured surface and gently knead until a dough ball forms.

Adding a little more flour as needed, roll the dough out into a rectangle, roughly 8 by 11 inches. Starting with a short end, fold the rectangle into thirds, like a letter. Wrap in parchment and refrigerate for 30 minutes.

Remove the dough from the refrigerator and roll out again into another roughly 8-by-11-inch rectangle. Using a cheese grater, grate the remaining 6 tablespoons of butter in an even layer over the surface of the dough. Fold the dough into thirds again, pinching the ends closed to trap the butter. Roll the dough out again and fold into thirds. Wrap the dough in parchment and chill for at least 30 minutes before using.

The dough can be stored in the refrigerator for up to 3 days before using or frozen for up to 1 month.

Lemon-Chive Vinaigrette

When life gives you lemons, you make lemonade. That's a saying, right? Eh, I can't remember the last time we made something as boring or basic as a plain old lemonade at the Independence or the Dragonfly Inn. (Although, I do dimly recall Lorelai using a paper cup of dollar lemonade to solve a teensy brûlée debacle at a Chilton bake sale . . . maybe that was Rory's first year? It was fine, no one was hurt, and we sold a lot of pastries that day.)

Well, when life gives *me* lemons—or specifically, when Jackson grows a signature crop of his famous Meyer lemons—*I* make Lemon-Chive Vinaigrette. First of all, it's a lot less antisocial than scaring people with your superhuman produce. Second, it goes with *everything*—I mean it. From salads to marinades, this one's a winner. Add a touch of garlic and honey for depth.

Yield: About 1¼ cups
V+*, GF

- ⅓ cup Meyer Lemon–Infused Vinegar (page 19)
- 1 small clove garlic, pressed or grated
- 1 tablespoon finely minced shallot (about ½ shallot)
- 1 to 2 tablespoons honey or maple syrup, divided
- ⅔ to 1 cup extra-virgin olive oil
- ¼ teaspoon sea salt
- Freshly ground black pepper
- ¼ cup finely chopped fresh chives

In a medium bowl, whisk the vinegar, garlic, shallot, and 1 tablespoon of the honey. Whisking constantly, slowly add in the oil, tasting until you reach your preferred oil-to-vinegar balance and the dressing has emulsified. Add the salt, pepper to taste, and more honey if desired. Transfer to a 12- to 16-ounce jar, add the chives, and shake until combined. Use immediately or store, refrigerated, for up to 1 week. Bring back to room temperature and shake before each use.

NOTE: This recipe is vegan if you use maple syrup instead of honey.

Speaking of that bake sale, ask Sookie—new cooking torch? —Lorelai

Chapter Two: Breakfast

Yield: 2 omelets
GF

- 2 ounces pancetta, diced, divided
- 2 tablespoons olive oil, divided
- 4 teaspoons dry sherry, divided
- 6 eggs, at room temperature, divided
- 2 tablespoons half-and-half, divided
- Freshly ground black pepper
- 2 ounces chèvre, divided

"I Have My Standards" Omelets

Word to the wise: Never take advice about your breakfast choices from someone who counts the blueberries in their morning muesli. That's just common sense. Egg whites are . . . fine, okay. Healthy, if you insist. Great source of protein! But there's more to life than protein, people! I mean, have we forgotten about flavor? About taste? Okay, if you want to be like Kirk and try to get that hearty, just-worked-out glow (without actually working out, obviously) then yes, the white of the egg is the way.

But if you're looking for deliciousness (yes, please!), here's the secret: three eggs. Yolks included. And my never-fail favorite add-in: pork. Yep, in the form of pancetta. Add some goat cheese? Hey, that's not a baa-d idea, either. It won't kill you. And a world without bacon or cheese in my omelet? Well, that's no way to live.

Your puns are as horrifying as your diet. —Michel

In a small skillet over medium heat, cook the pancetta until most of the fat has rendered and it's browning, about 5 minutes. Remove from the pan and drain on paper towels until needed.

In a small bowl, whisk together 1 tablespoon of the olive oil and 2 teaspoons of the sherry.

In a large bowl, whisk together 3 of the eggs, 1 tablespoon of the half-and-half, and pepper to taste until homogenized with no streaks of egg white or egg yolk showing.

In an 8-inch egg pan over medium heat, add the oil mixture. When the oil spreads over the surface of the pan, add the egg mixture. With a wooden spoon, start to stir the eggs immediately while shaking the pan. Keep agitating the eggs until most of the mixture has formed into curds. Shake the pan to settle the curds and use the spoon to fill any holes in the egg mixture. Working quickly, add half the pancetta and half the chèvre in a strip down the center of the pan. Have a plate ready and use a thin spatula to lift the edges of the omelet. Remove the pan from the heat, tilt it toward the plate, and use the spatula to roll the omelet onto the plate.

Serve immediately. Repeat for the second omelet.

Yield: 1 omelet
V, GF

- 2 large mushrooms (about 2 ounces)
- 3 teaspoons olive oil, divided
- 3 egg whites
- 2 teaspoons snipped chives, divided
- ¼ teaspoon salt
- Freshly ground black pepper
- 3 or 4 cherry tomatoes, quartered

Healthy (Boring) Egg-White Omelet

Okay, fine, if you insist on being virtuous and heart-healthy and eschewing the egg yolk, I've got you. If anyone can make a delicious egg-white omelet, I'm your girl. The key is fresh herbs and veggies, and you know I'm all over that. Hey, here's a fun thought—why not make it a game? Whip up one of each style omelet, yolked and white, and have yourself a battle of the breakfasts? There could be custom T-shirts! You could keep score! The Ultimate Egg-cellent Omelet Throwdown? How very Stars Hollow of you.

Remove the stems from the mushrooms, discard, and thinly slice the mushroom caps. In a small skillet over medium heat, heat 2 teaspoons of the oil and sauté the mushrooms until browned and tender, about 5 minutes. Transfer to a plate and set aside.

Prepare an egg pan with the remaining 1 teaspoon of oil.

In a large bowl, to give you plenty of whisking room, combine the egg whites, 1 teaspoon of the chives, the salt, and pepper to taste and whisk vigorously until very foamy and opaque, up to 3 minutes.

Heat the egg pan over medium heat, and when the oil spreads across the pan, give the eggs a few more whisks, then add them to the pan.

Immediately stir the eggs with a wooden spoon while shaking the pan. Keep agitating the eggs until most of the mixture has formed into curds. Shake the pan to settle the curds and use the spoon to fill any holes in the egg mixture. Add the mushrooms down the center of the pan. Use a thin spatula to lift the edges of the omelet. Remove the pan from the heat, tilt it toward a plate, and use the spatula to roll the omelet onto the plate. Sprinkle with the remaining 1 teaspoon of chives and top with the tomatoes. Serve immediately.

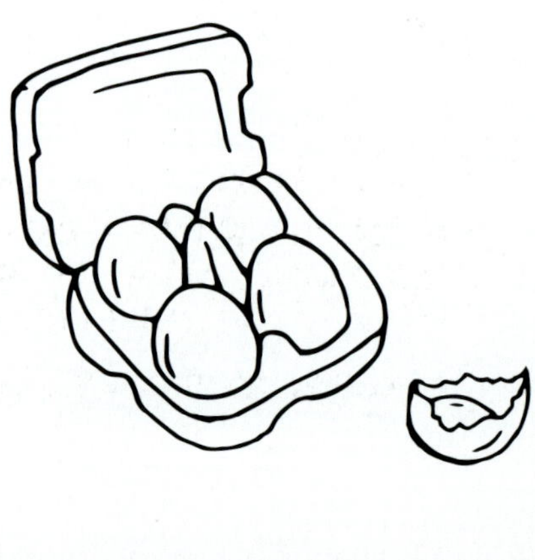

Blueberry-Lemon Pancakes

We've already talked about making lemonade from lemons, so we don't need to go there again. Instead, let's say when your produce supplier gives you blueberries and you allow yourself to eat more than eight at a time (ahem, Michel), you may as well make a heaping stack of these.

Pancakes won't solve all your problems, but they sure are tasty! Especially my famous blueberry-lemon pancakes. They feature Jackson's famous Meyer lemons, of which—you may have heard—we had a bumper crop this year. Fluffy, buttery, and zesty, these pancakes are always a hit. They were a mainstay at the Independence Inn, we served them to a very accommodating crowd at Luke's Diner one day in a pinch, and of course, they're the star of the weekend brunch menu at the Dragonfly. A great option for a buffet alongside Belgian Waffles with Famous Peach Sauce (page 34). In this case, we ditch the maple syrup for a lemon ricotta. (Trust me, you're gonna plotz.)

Yield: 10 to 12 pancakes; 1 cup berry compote
V

BLUEBERRY COMPOTE:

- 1 cup frozen wild blueberries
- ½ cup granulated sugar
- 1 Meyer lemon, juice and zest divided (about ¼ cup of juice)
- ¼ cup water

PANCAKES:

- 16 ounces whole-milk ricotta cheese
- Zest from the above lemon (about 1 teaspoon)
- 2 large eggs
- 2 tablespoons granulated sugar
- 1 cup all-purpose flour
- ¼ teaspoon kosher salt
- 2 teaspoons baking powder
- ⅛ teaspoon allspice
- Up to ½ cup milk (depending on the ricotta's moisture level)
- Butter, for serving

TO MAKE THE BLUEBERRY COMPOTE: In a medium saucepan over medium heat, combine the blueberries, sugar, lemon juice, and water until the sugar is dissolved. Bring to a boil and then reduce to a simmer for 10 to 15 minutes or until the syrup coats the back of the mixing spoon. Remove from the heat and allow to cool while making the pancakes.

TO MAKE THE PANCAKES: In the bowl of a food processor, pulse the ricotta, lemon zest, eggs, and sugar until completely smooth, scraping down the sides of the bowl at least once. Turn off the processor and allow the mixture to rest during the next step.

In a large bowl, mix the flour, salt, baking powder, and allspice.

Stir the ricotta mixture into the flour mixture. If the batter is too thick, slowly add the milk, 2 or 3 tablespoons at a time, until the batter ribbons off the spatula similar to regular pancake batter.

Preheat a large skillet over medium-high heat and preheat the oven to 250°F.

Using a scant ½ cup of batter per pancake, cook each pancake until the batter around the edges begins to bubble, 2 to 3 minutes. Gently flip and brown on the other side, about 2 minutes. Transfer to a plate or baking sheet in the oven and allow each pancake to rest for 3 to 5 minutes before serving. This will help the centers cook and firm up a bit more.

Serve the pancakes hot with butter and warm blueberry compote.

Belgian Waffles with Famous Peach Sauce

Maybe my second-favorite import from Belgium, after that salad bowl that I "donated" (not by choice) to an ill-fated deep-fried Thanksgiving dinner, these waffles are a mainstay on the Dragonfly brunch menu. If you tried the Blueberry-Lemon Pancakes (page 33), you know Chef Sookie doesn't waste time with garden-variety maple syrup. These are served with my signature Famous Peach Sauce (page 14) that was so spectacular, Lorelai debated bathing in it. (Don't worry, she didn't. Which was probably the right call, knowing how Luke feels about kids and their sticky "jam hands.")

Yield: About eight 7-inch waffles
V

SPECIAL TOOL:
- Kitchen thermometer

- 3 cups milk, at room temperature, divided
- 4 tablespoons granulated sugar, divided
- 1 envelope (2¼ teaspoons) active dry yeast
- ½ cup (8 tablespoons) unsalted butter, plus more for serving
- 3 eggs, separated
- 4 tablespoons crème fraîche, plus more for serving
- 1 teaspoon salt
- 2 teaspoons vanilla paste
- 4 cups all-purpose flour
- ½ teaspoon ground cinnamon

In a heatproof measuring cup or bowl, heat ¼ cup of the milk to between 110°F and 115°F, add 1 teaspoon of the sugar, and stir to dissolve. Sprinkle the yeast over the top, stir gently, and set aside for 5 minutes or until foamy.

In another heatproof measuring cup, melt the butter with another ¼ cup of milk, allow to cool slightly, and whisk in the egg yolks and 4 tablespoons of crème fraîche until smooth. Add the yeast mixture, remaining sugar, salt, and vanilla paste. Whisk until smooth.

In a large bowl, combine the flour and cinnamon. Add the butter mixture, stir gently until a shaggy dough forms, and slowly add the remaining 2½ cups of milk in about ½-cup additions, stirring in between each addition. Continue to stir until all the flour has been incorporated.

In a medium bowl, beat the egg whites until soft peaks form and gently fold them into the batter.

Cover the bowl tightly with plastic wrap and put in a proofing oven or warm place to rise for 1 hour or until doubled in size.

Once the batter has risen, gently punch it down with a wooden spoon and stir it once. Make the waffles with the batter according to your waffle maker's instructions. Serve immediately with Famous Peach Sauce (page 14) and a dollop of crème fraîche, if using. The waffles can also be buttered before serving, if desired.

TIP: This batter can be made a day ahead, covered tightly with plastic wrap, and refrigerated overnight. Allow to finish the rise in a warm place for 1 to 1½ hours or until it has doubled in size.

Don't forget the toast points!

Shirred Eggs with Chive

I'm a chef. It's who I am. It's in my blood. (Probably not literally . . . but then again, with all the kitchen accidents, who even knows?) When I've got no kitchen or chance to cook, my skills . . . they . . . they deteriorate! I need to cook! I need to sauté, emulsify, marinate. I need to fry a frickin' dead animal in a skillet. You get it.

In summary, if I go too long without a kitchen, very bad things happen. My whole body gets itchy and weird and antsy, like I just ate some dark chocolate and drank an espresso.

Now, these eggs don't qualify as "dead animal" per se, but this recipe did scratch the itch during the previously mentioned Dragonfly Inn kitchen fire. I put Luke on chive duty (he loved it). Don't forget toast points for sopping up the extra sauce.

LOVE IS A STRONG WORD.
—LUKE

Yield: 4 servings
V, GF*

SPECIAL TOOLS:

- Four 6-ounce ramekins

TOAST POINTS:

- 2 tablespoons unsalted butter
- 6 slices white bread
- Salt
- Freshly ground black pepper

CHIVE-INFUSED CREAM:

- 1 cup heavy cream
- ¼ cup coarsely chopped chives, plus more for garnish
- 1 large or 2 small cloves garlic, halved

SHIRRED EGGS:

- 2 teaspoons salted butter, softened
- ½ cup Chive-Infused Cream
- 8 eggs
- Salt
- Freshly ground black pepper

TO MAKE THE TOAST POINTS: Preheat the oven to 400°F.

In a small bowl, microwave the butter until just melted, 10 to 15 seconds.

Cut the crusts from the bread slices. Coat one side of each bread slice with the butter. Sprinkle a pinch of salt and pepper evenly across each slice. Cut the bread in half into triangles. Place the triangles, butter-side up, on a baking sheet. Bake for 5 to 7 minutes, or until golden. Allow to cool for 30 minutes while you make the cream and eggs.

TO MAKE THE CHIVE-INFUSED CREAM: In a small saucepan over medium-low heat, bring the cream, chives, and garlic to a simmer. Reduce the heat to low and cook, stirring often, for 10 minutes. Set aside for 10 minutes to continue steeping. Strain the cream through a fine-mesh strainer into a bowl, discarding the solids.

TO MAKE THE SHIRRED EGGS: Preheat the oven to 325°F.

Grease each 6-ounce ramekin lightly with the butter. Place 3 tablespoons of the infused cream into each ramekin. Crack 2 eggs into each ramekin, being careful not to break the yolk. Alternatively, crack the eggs into a small bowl and slide them into the ramekin. Sprinkle each with a pinch of salt and pepper. Place the ramekins on a baking sheet and bake for 15 to 18 minutes, or until the whites have set but the yolks are still soft. Remove from the oven and allow to sit for 2 to 3 minutes. Garnish with chives and serve immediately with the toast points.

NOTE: This recipe can be made gluten free by choosing gluten-free bread for making the toast points.

Yield: 8 scones
V

SPECIAL TOOL:

- Pastry cutter

- ½ cup currants
- Zest and 1 tablespoon juice from 1 orange, divided
- About 1 cup boiling water
- 2 cups all-purpose flour
- ¼ cup granulated sugar
- 1 tablespoon baking powder
- ¼ teaspoon salt
- ¼ teaspoon ground cloves
- 6 tablespoons unsalted butter, very cold
- ½ cup plus 1 teaspoon heavy whipping cream, divided
- 1 egg
- ½ cup powdered sugar
- ¼ teaspoon ground cinnamon

Currant and Spice Scones

We always have a selection of fresh-baked scones available at the Dragonfly. Richard noticed their divine scent when he first came to visit Lorelai in Stars Hollow. Naturally, I sent him home with six months' supply. Now, that's just the normal amount to keep on hand in case of a scone emergency. Haven't you ever done that? Got caught up in something that snowballs into a whole personality? Like when Jackson and I first started dating, we went to this pickle festival. He wore a shirt with a frog on it.

So I said, "Hey, cute frog." And he goes, "Oh, you like frogs?" And I said yes, because—right? So then for our six-month anniversary, he got me a frog figurine. Fast-forward to today and I'm Frog Girl. Frog Girl. Frog hoarder, more like. Don't be Frog-Hoarder Person. Be better. Be Scone-Hoarder Person. Just for the extra shelf space alone! You'll need those shelves for all your scones.

Line a baking sheet with a silicone baking mat or parchment paper and preheat the oven to 425°F.

In a heatproof bowl or measuring cup, combine the currants and orange zest. Pour the boiling water over the top of the mixture until the currants are just covered, and stir to combine. Allow to steep for 5 minutes. Drain the currants and orange zest, discarding the liquid, and set aside.

In a large bowl, combine the flour, granulated sugar, baking powder, salt, and cloves. Add the currants and orange zest. Stir to evenly distribute the currants. Using a pastry cutter or two knives, cut the butter into the flour until the butter pieces are the size of peas.

In a small bowl or measuring cup, whisk together ½ cup of the whipping cream and the egg. Using a rubber spatula, stir the cream mixture into the flour mixture until a shaggy dough forms. Gently knead the final bits of flour into the dough.

Turn the dough out onto the prepared baking sheet and gently form into a circle about 6 inches in diameter and about 1 inch thick. Cut the circle into eight equal triangles by cutting it directly in half and then cutting each piece in half and then in half again.

In the same bowl that you whisked the cream and egg in, add the remaining 1 teaspoon of whipping cream and ½ teaspoon of the reserved orange juice. Stir together and brush the top of each scone.

Bake for 10 to 12 minutes, or until golden brown. Allow to cool on the baking sheet.

While the scones are cooling, prepare a glaze by whisking together the remaining 2½ teaspoons of orange juice, the powdered sugar, and the cinnamon in a small mixing bowl. When the scones are cool to the touch, drizzle the glaze over them. Allow to set for 2 to 3 minutes and serve immediately.

Scones are best fresh, but they can be stored in an airtight container for up to 3 days.

Muffin Tops Two Ways

As many of you may (or should) know, the tastiest part of the muffin is the top. This isn't up for debate, unless you want to be the one to take it up with Lorelai.

A big basket of these muffin tops is my very favorite bribe . . . er, expression of love and gratitude. I do have a little good news/bad news situation for you about the double-chocolate chip muffin tops, though: They're more like cake than muffins. Spongy and rich and studded with so many chips, you could break a tooth.

But if calling them a muffin means you can eat them in the morning, I'm all for it. Go forth and chocolate morning cake in good health (and uncracked teeth!).

Yield: 11 of each flavor
V

DOUBLE-CHOCOLATE CHIP MUFFINS:

- Coconut oil, for greasing
- 1¾ cups all-purpose flour, divided
- 1 teaspoon baking soda
- 1 teaspoon baking powder
- ¼ cup unsweetened cocoa powder
- ½ cup (8 tablespoons) salted butter, softened
- ½ cup granulated sugar
- 2 large eggs, at room temperature
- 1 teaspoon vanilla extract
- ½ cup sour cream
- ½ cup very hot water
- 1 cup semisweet chocolate chips

Ingredients continue on page 42

TO MAKE THE DOUBLE-CHOCOLATE CHIP MUFFINS: Preheat the oven to 425°F. Grease just the top of a 12-capacity muffin tin around each cavity with coconut oil. Line with paper muffin liners.

In a medium bowl, combine 1½ cups of the flour, the baking soda, baking powder, and cocoa powder. Set aside.

Fit a stand mixer with a paddle attachment or use a large mixing bowl if using a hand mixer. Put the butter and sugar in the bowl and beat on high speed until light and fluffy, about 2 minutes. Add the eggs one at a time and mix on medium speed between each addition. Add the vanilla and mix again.

Add half of the flour mixture and mix on low speed to incorporate, scraping down the sides of the bowl as needed. Add the sour cream, mixing on low speed to combine. Add the rest of the flour mixture and mix on low speed again. Once everything is incorporated, with the mixer on low speed, drizzle in the water and continue to mix until completely incorporated. Scrape down the bowl as needed.

In a small mixing bowl, mix the chocolate chips with the remaining ¼ cup of flour and then fold them into the batter. Use an ice-cream scoop to fill each muffin cavity almost all the way to the top. To create a big "muffin top," we fill these more than the common two-thirds.

Bake for 5 minutes. Without opening the oven, reduce the temperature to 350°F and bake for another 12 to 15 minutes or until the cake tester comes out clean. Allow to cool in the pan set on a wire rack. To remove the top for a muffin top–only serving, use your fingers to gently pull each top away from the base and serve. Store the bottoms in an airtight container and use for Muffin Bottom Meringue and Ice-Cream Pie (page 152).

APPLE-CINNAMON WALNUT MUFFINS:

- Coconut oil, for greasing
- 1 tablespoon apple cider vinegar
- 1 medium apple, peeled, cored, and diced
- 1¾ cups all-purpose flour, divided
- 1 teaspoon baking soda
- 1 teaspoon baking powder
- ½ teaspoon salt
- 1 teaspoon ground cinnamon, divided
- ½ teaspoon ground nutmeg
- ½ cup (8 tablespoons) salted butter, softened
- ½ cup packed dark brown sugar
- ¼ cup plus 1 tablespoon granulated sugar, divided
- 2 large eggs, at room temperature
- ½ cup applesauce
- 1 cup toasted walnut pieces

TO MAKE THE APPLE-CINNAMON WALNUT MUFFINS: Preheat the oven to 425°F. Grease just the top of a 12-capacity muffin tin around each cavity with coconut oil. Line with paper muffin liners.

Pour the vinegar into a small bowl. Add the apple pieces to the vinegar and set aside.

In a medium bowl, add 1½ cups of the flour, the baking soda, baking powder, salt, ½ teaspoon of the cinnamon, and the nutmeg; stir to combine. Set aside.

Fit a stand mixer with a paddle attachment or use a large mixing bowl if using a hand mixer. Put the butter, brown sugar, and ¼ cup of the granulated sugar in the bowl and beat on high speed until light and fluffy, about 2 minutes. Add the eggs one at a time and mix on medium speed between each addition.

Add half of the flour mixture and mix on low speed to incorporate, scraping down the sides of the bowl as needed. Add the applesauce, mixing on low speed to combine. Add the rest of the flour mixture and mix on low speed again. In a mixing bowl, toss the apples and walnuts in the remaining ¼ cup of flour and fold into the batter. Use an ice-cream scoop to fill each muffin cavity almost all the way to the top. To create a big "muffin top" we fill these more than the common two-thirds.

In a small bowl, mix the remaining ½ teaspoon of cinnamon with the remaining 1 tablespoon of granulated sugar and sprinkle on the top of each muffin.

Bake for 5 minutes. Without opening the oven, reduce the temperature to 350°F and bake for another 12 to 15 minutes or until the cake tester comes out clean. Allow to cool in the pan set on a wire rack. To remove the top for a muffin top–only serving, use your fingers to gently pull each top away from the base and serve. Store the bottoms in an airtight container and use for Muffin Bottom Meringue and Ice-Cream Pie (see page 152).

TIP: Feel free to serve the muffins whole; just be aware that certain besties may leave the bottoms behind!

Orange-Glazed Muffins with Warm Cinnamon Butter

What did one orange say to the other orange?

If you weren't so fresh, we wouldn't be in this jam!

Ba dump-tss.

That's Martha's favorite joke. I put it in at her request. Yes, I am fully aware there's a world of difference between a glaze and a jam (do not get me started, and if you value your limbs, don't even mention the subject of jelly, either). You try telling your kid their joke won't make it into your official cookbook.

But for the love of jeepers, please don't tell her what Jackson and I were actually doing that time Lorelai caught us in the Dragonfly kitchen discussing "jam making." There's a whole world out there beyond growing vegetables, and I'm just not ready for that conversation yet!

Yield: 12 muffins
V

MUFFINS:

- Butter, for greasing
- 1 cup rolled oats
- 1½ cups all-purpose flour
- ¼ cup wheat germ
- 1 teaspoon kosher salt
- 1 tablespoon baking powder
- ¼ teaspoon ground cloves
- 2 eggs
- ⅔ cup packed light brown sugar
- 1 cup whole milk, at room temperature
- ½ cup (8 tablespoons) unsalted butter, melted
- ¼ cup plus 2 tablespoons orange marmalade, divided

CINNAMON BUTTER:

- ½ cup (8 tablespoons) salted butter, softened
- 1 teaspoon granulated sugar
- 1 teaspoon ground cinnamon

TO MAKE THE MUFFINS: Preheat the oven to 400°F. Grease the top of a 12-capacity muffin tin and line with muffin liners.

In a large bowl, combine the oats, flour, wheat germ, salt, baking powder, and cloves. In a separate large bowl, combine the eggs, brown sugar, milk, and butter and whisk thoroughly. Add the egg mixture to the oats mixture and stir quickly to combine. Let rest for 15 minutes, then stir in ¼ cup of the marmalade.

Scoop the batter into the muffin liners, filling almost to the top. Bake for 5 minutes and, without opening the oven, reduce the temperature to 350°F and bake for another 10 to 12 minutes or until a cake tester comes out clean.

While the muffins are baking, whisk the remaining 2 tablespoons of marmalade with a fork.

TO MAKE THE CINNAMON BUTTER: In a small bowl, combine the butter, sugar, and cinnamon, then transfer to a serving dish.

While the muffins are still hot, use a pastry brush to coat the top of each one with the marmalade and allow to cool until the glaze is set, about 5 minutes. Serve warm or at room temperature with the cinnamon butter.

The muffins and butter can be stored in an airtight container at room temperature for up to 3 days.

Luke's Diner Cajun Eggs Benedict

Yield: 4 to 8 servings

SPECIAL TOOLS:

- Box grater
- 2½-inch round biscuit cutter

CORNMEAL BISCUITS:

- 2 cups all-purpose flour, plus more for the work surface
- 1 tablespoon baking powder
- ½ teaspoon baking soda
- ½ teaspoon salt
- 10 tablespoons unsalted or salted butter, preferably European style, frozen
- 1 cup yellow or white medium-grind cornmeal (see note)
- 1 cup buttermilk
- 2 tablespoons maple syrup

Ingredients continue on page 46

NOTE: Medium-grind cornmeal provides a wonderful texture for the biscuits if you are able to find it. A fine grind will give you a more tender biscuit.

This recipe is proof that I do know how to delegate, under the right circumstances—for example, when there's been a fire at the inn and I need to play nice(ish) with Luke if I want access to his kitchen to make breakfast for our guests. And believe it or not, Mr. "No-one-comes-behind-my-counter-but-me" can be persuaded to cooperate, too.

It turns out we make a pretty good team. His regulars loved my Blueberry-Lemon Pancakes (page 33), and together we invented a spicy spin on your boring old basic eggs Benedict. Did it happen when someone accidentally knocked a bottle of hot sauce over into a pan of eggs? Maybe. Does it matter if we "meant" it, if it was a happy (and delicious) outcome? Nope.

In this version, which I've tweaked since then, Cajun hollandaise gives this dish a kick instead of a bottle of hot sauce; add grilled shrimp to be extra fancy-pants. (Blackened if you're looking to up the "BAM!" factor.)

TO MAKE THE CORNMEAL BISCUITS: In a large bowl, whisk the flour, baking powder, baking soda, and salt. Using the large hole-side of a box grater, grate the butter into the flour mixture. Use a fork to toss the butter in evenly. Make a well in the center of the flour mixture.

In a medium bowl, whisk the cornmeal, buttermilk, and maple syrup. Add the cornmeal mixture into the well and stir with the fork until it just comes together.

Turn the dough out onto a lightly floured work surface. Using your hands, gently work the dough to bring it together, adding a little flour if too wet. Wrap the dough in plastic wrap and let it sit at room temperature for 15 minutes.

Line a baking sheet with parchment paper. Roll the dough out to about 1 inch thick. Use the biscuit cutter to cut as many biscuits as possible, reforming the dough as needed. Put the biscuits on the prepared baking sheet and place in the freezer for 10 minutes. Preheat the oven to 450°F.

Remove the biscuits from the freezer and bake for 5 minutes. Reduce the temperature to 400°F and bake for another 8 to 10 minutes, or until puffed and golden. Place the baking sheet on a wire rack to cool.

CAJUN HOLLANDAISE:

- ½ cup (8 tablespoons) salted butter
- 2 egg yolks, at room temperature
- 2 teaspoons lemon juice
- ¼ teaspoon kosher salt
- ¼ teaspoon smoked paprika
- ⅛ teaspoon cayenne pepper
- ⅛ teaspoon garlic powder
- ¼ teaspoon dried oregano

EGGS BENEDICT:

- 8 strips bacon
- 16 large shrimp, peeled and deveined (about 8 ounces)
- ⅛ teaspoon salt, plus more as needed
- ⅛ teaspoon black pepper, plus more as needed
- ¼ teaspoon smoked paprika
- ⅛ teaspoon cayenne pepper (optional)
- ¼ teaspoon garlic powder
- 8 eggs
- 4 cornmeal biscuits or toasted English muffins
- 2 tablespoons chopped chives, for garnish

TO MAKE THE CAJUN HOLLANDAISE: In a small bowl, covered, melt the butter in a microwave for about 1 minute, or until hot. In a blender, pulse the egg yolks, lemon juice, salt, paprika, cayenne pepper, garlic powder, and oregano on low speed for 10 seconds. With the blender running on medium-high speed, slowly stream in the hot butter until the mixture has blended into a creamy sauce, or emulsified.

TO MAKE THE EGGS BENEDICT: Line a plate with paper towels. In a large heavy skillet over medium heat, cook the bacon for 5 minutes, or until golden brown. Using tongs, transfer the bacon to the prepared plate and set aside, reserving the skillet with the bacon grease.

Fill a medium saucepan with several inches of water. Over medium-high heat, bring the water to a gentle simmer. While the water is coming to a simmer, put the shrimp in a medium bowl and pat dry with paper towels. Add the salt, black pepper, smoked paprika, cayenne pepper (if using), and garlic powder, tossing to distribute the spices evenly.

Once the water is simmering, reduce the heat to medium-low. Crack the eggs, one at a time, into a small cup or bowl and slip the eggs into the simmering water. Continue to cook at a very low simmer for 3 to 5 minutes, turning the eggs occasionally with a slotted spoon, until the whites are set. With a slotted spoon, transfer the eggs to a large plate and set aside.

In the skillet with the bacon grease, over medium heat, add the shrimp and cook for about 2 minutes per side, or until the shrimp are just cooked. Use a slotted spoon or tongs to transfer the shrimp to a plate.

To serve, split the biscuits in half. Place both halves, cut-side up, on four plates, or one half on eight plates, or a serving platter. Cut each piece of bacon in half and place two halves on each biscuit. Top the bacon with one egg. Spoon the hollandaise sauce over each egg and top with two shrimp. Sprinkle the chives over the shrimp and serve immediately.

TIP: To create a velvety-smooth sauce, your butter needs to be hot as you add it to the other ingredients in the blender. If your sauce separates, slowly stream in 1 (or up to 2) tablespoon of boiling hot water while the blender is running at medium-high speed.

Caramelized Hazelnut Brioche French Toast

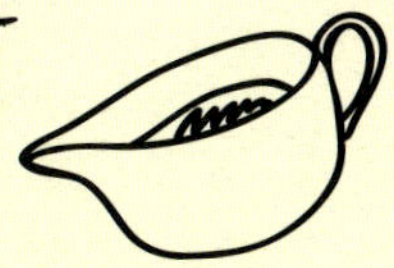

Wasn't it Chekhov who said, "If you introduce the Homemade Brioche Bread (page 10) in the first section of the cookbook, it needs to come back in the last section"? Well, if he didn't say that, he should have! Think of this as Chekov's French toast.

(If you <u>must</u> buy store-bought brioche, I'll allow it. But let me tell you, you're missing out. The first time I made bread from scratch was <u>so</u> exciting. Like the day you get your Spanish name in Spanish class. Not diminished at all by the fact that they kind of had to make up a Spanish name for me—<u>Sookia</u>. <u>Señora Sookia</u> to you.)

Caramelized hazelnuts give this a little extra oomph (Luke had his doubts, too, but I showed him). Fluffy, airy, crunchy, sweet . . . I'm not kidding when I say Luke and I just may be on track to win a Nobel prize for this collaboration. Chekov would be so proud.

Yield: 8 slices (4 servings)
V

CARAMELIZED HAZELNUTS:

- ½ cup roasted, unsalted hazelnuts
- ¾ cup granulated sugar
- ¼ cup water

Ingredients continue on page 48

TO MAKE THE CARAMELIZED HAZELNUTS: Measure out the hazelnuts in a small bowl. Line a rimmed baking sheet with a silicone baking mat or parchment paper.

Carefully pour the sugar into a small, heavy-bottomed saucepan with a tight-fitting lid, keeping it as centered as possible. Put the pan on the stove over medium-high heat and carefully pour the water around the edge of the sugar. Use a high-heat rubber spatula or a wooden spoon to slowly draw the water from the edge of the pan through the sugar to moisten it without stirring. Continue to gently pull the water back and forth without stirring; you don't want to splash any sugar crystals on the side of the pan. Cook until the sugar has dissolved, never stirring, but continuing to draw the water gently back and forth. Once the sugar has dissolved, let the mixture boil, cover with the lid, and boil for 2 minutes.

Carefully remove the lid, watch for steam, and swirl the pan gently. Continue to cook, swirling occasionally, until the sugar has reached a deep amber color, 3 to 5 minutes. Once the sugar has caramelized, immediately remove it from the heat and stir in half the hazelnuts. Use a fork to remove one or two hazelnuts at a time, allowing the excess caramel to drip off, and put them on the prepared baking sheet. Continue until you have covered all the hazelnuts, adding the second half when you are done with the first. If the syrup gets too thick to work with, return it to the stove over low heat and swirl until pliable.

Once all the hazelnuts are covered, use the fork to drizzle the rest of the caramel over the nuts, creating fine threads. You may not use all the caramel (stop when the sheet is covered in threads).

FRENCH TOAST:

- 1 loaf Homemade Brioche Bread (page 10) or store-bought
- 1½ cups half-and-half
- 1½ tablespoons espresso powder
- 1½ tablespoons granulated sugar
- 1 tablespoon vanilla extract
- ¼ teaspoon salt
- 10 tablespoons unsalted butter, divided
- 6 eggs
- ½ cup raw or turbinado sugar

COFFEE SYRUP (OPTIONAL):

- 1 cup coffee
- ½ cup raw or turbinado sugar

NOTE: If you are cooking to order, the toast can be served after 5 minutes in the oven.

The sugar should set and cool in 5 to 10 minutes. Once it is cool, break the threads apart, creating decorative shards (some nuts may break apart and be on their own), and store them in an airtight container between layers of parchment paper. These can be made up to 3 days ahead if kept in a cool, dry place.

TO MAKE THE FRENCH TOAST: Preheat the oven to 300°F and put a rimmed baking sheet, fitted with a wire rack, inside.

Cut the loaf of brioche into eight thick slices and use a fork to poke holes in the surface of each slice. Set aside.

In a baking dish large enough to hold two pieces of brioche, combine the half-and-half, espresso powder, granulated sugar, vanilla, and salt and whisk until the espresso powder is dissolved. In a small microwave-safe bowl, melt 6 tablespoons of the butter in the microwave for about 30 seconds (or more if needed) and add to the mixture, whisking to combine. Add the eggs one at a time, whisking after each addition, until well combined, creating a custard.

Working with two pieces of bread at a time, soak them in the custard on both sides until they are well saturated but still holding together. While the pieces are soaking, heat a skillet large enough to hold two pieces of bread at a time over medium-high heat and add 1 tablespoon of butter. When the butter begins to foam, add the bread slices. Cook until the pieces will move freely when you gently shake the pan, 2 to 3 minutes. Sprinkle the exposed, uncooked sides with 1½ teaspoons of the raw sugar on each piece. Flip the bread and sprinkle the cooked side with another 1½ teaspoons of raw sugar for each piece. Continue to cook for 2 to 3 minutes or until you begin to see caramelized sugar oozing out from under the bread pieces. Flip again and caramelize the sugar on the other side. Transfer to the baking sheet in the oven and repeat three more times with the remaining slices.

TO MAKE THE OPTIONAL COFFEE SYRUP: Deglaze the pan in which you cooked the caramel with the coffee, scraping the pan with a spoon to loosen any flavorful bits, add the raw sugar, and simmer until the sugar is dissolved and the syrup begins to thicken. Strain through a fine-mesh strainer into a small pitcher or cup, discarding the solids.

To serve, put two pieces of French toast on a plate, and decorate with the candied hazelnuts and caramel shards. If you have made the syrup, let guests add it themselves.

Chapter Three: Starters

Chicken Taquito Blinis with Avocado Crema

What makes these taquito blinis as opposed to plain old, regular taquitos? I'm so glad you asked! The secret is: It's all in your attitude! (Well, and also a few eensy tweaks and garnishes with high-end or unexpected ingredients. If we're being picky.) A last-minute dinner party calls for a menu that's fun and filled with whimsy—and festive finger food! ("Fun-filled festive finger food!" Try saying that one five times fast!)

But when that dinner party includes your extremely formal, extra-fastidious parents? As Lorelai herself might say, "Oy with the poodles already!" (It's a very all-purpose catchphrase; give it a whirl.) I first made these for what I thought was a Lorelai-Rory-mother-daughter-junk-food-and-hang. Once I found out Richard and Emily were coming, I punted. Boy oh boy, did I punt . . . Now you can try my extremely fancy-pants interpretation of a snack attack classic. Olé!

Yield: About 30 taquitos

SPECIAL TOOL:

- Kitchen thermometer

PULLED CHICKEN:

- 2 pounds boneless, skinless chicken thighs (about 6 pieces)
- 2 tablespoons olive oil
- 1 tablespoon smoked paprika
- ¼ teaspoon chili powder
- 2 teaspoons ground cumin
- 1 teaspoon kosher salt
- 3 cloves garlic, finely minced
- Juice from 2 limes (about ¼ cup)

AVOCADO CREMA:

- 2 avocados
- ¼ cup chopped cilantro
- 1 cup sour cream
- ½ teaspoon kosher salt
- Juice from 2 limes (about ¼ cup)
- 2 cloves garlic, minced
- 1 tablespoon canned diced green chiles

Ingredients continue on page 54

TO MAKE THE PULLED CHICKEN: In a large glass bowl or baking dish, combine the chicken, oil, paprika, chili powder, cumin, salt, garlic, and lime juice. Cover tightly with plastic wrap and refrigerate for at least 2 hours or overnight.

Preheat the oven to 350°F.

Put the chicken in a Dutch oven, including all the marinade. Cover and bake for 40 to 50 minutes until fully cooked and fall-apart tender. (Alternatively, cook in a slow cooker on low for 6 hours, or until fork-tender.) Transfer each piece of chicken to a bowl and shred before returning back to the sauce. Allow to come to room temperature before proceeding, or store in an airtight container, refrigerated, for up to 3 days.

TO MAKE THE AVOCADO CREMA: Peel and remove the pit from the avocados. In a blender or food processor, pulse the avocado, cilantro, sour cream, salt, lime juice, and garlic until very smooth, scraping down the sides as needed. Add the green chiles and pulse once to combine. Serve immediately or transfer to an airtight container, placing a piece of plastic on the surface of the crema to prevent discoloration, and refrigerate for up to 3 days.

TAQUITOS:

- 2 cups pulled chicken (see note)
- 2 tablespoons canned diced green chiles
- 1 cup shredded sharp cheddar cheese
- Salt
- Freshly ground black pepper
- 30 round 3½-inch dumpling wrappers
- 2 to 4 cups avocado oil or other neutral oil, for frying

TO MAKE THE TAQUITOS: Pour ½ cup of water into a small bowl and set aside.

In a medium bowl, combine the chicken, chiles, and cheese. Add salt and pepper to taste. Working with one dumpling wrapper at a time, spoon about 1 tablespoon of filling into the middle of the wrapper. Spread the filling down the center in a line top to bottom, keeping the two sides free. Dip a finger in the water and wet one of the empty edges. Roll tightly toward the wet edge and place seam-side down on a baking sheet or plate. Continue building the taquitos.

Set a wire rack over a baking sheet and cover it with a paper towel. Pour 1½ inches of oil into a large frying pan over medium-high heat. Bring the oil to 350°F, or until the oil sizzles when you add your taquitos. Using tongs, fry several at a time without crowding them, turning them often, until they are crispy and golden brown. Put them on the wire rack, dusting with a pinch of salt, and continue frying the remaining taquitos. Serve warm with the avocado crema.

NOTE: You will have more chicken than you need. It freezes well for another batch of taquitos or can be used on its own or in quesadillas for another meal.

The Original Onion Dip

Do you know, I actually met someone the other day who had no idea that sour cream and onion potato chips were originally based on actual onion dip that people dipped chips and stuff into? Zero. Zip. Nada! Wild, right?

How do you get to grown-up age without getting the connection between onion-dip-flavored chips and the very dip they were first modeled after? How? Heck if I know.

No matter, I'm going to teach you how to make knock-'em-dead onion dip from scratch, in obscene, swimming-pool-size quantities. (No joke. After Rory's 16th, Lorelai was worried they'd be eating onion dip for breakfast for a week.) Freeze a batch for storage, then use the extras for a DIY home spa treatment . . .

. . . Or see my suggestion for mixing in ground turkey and garlic to give your leftovers (you will have leftovers) a new lease on life. Take a dip, why don't you?

Yield: 2¼ cups
V, GF

- 3 tablespoons unsalted butter
- 3 cups diced Vidalia or yellow onions (about 1¼ pounds or 2 or 3 onions)
- 1½ teaspoons kosher salt or ¾ teaspoon table salt, plus more as needed
- 1 tablespoon onion powder
- ½ teaspoon garlic powder
- ½ teaspoon white or black pepper, plus more as needed
- 2 cloves garlic, finely chopped
- 1 teaspoon ground cumin
- 1 cup sour cream
- ½ cup mayonnaise
- Chopped fresh chives or scallion greens, for garnish (optional)

In a large cast-iron or heavy-bottomed pan over medium heat, melt the butter. Add the onions, salt, onion powder, garlic powder, and pepper and stir until well combined. Sauté, stirring, for 5 minutes. Reduce the heat to medium-low and continue to cook, stirring occasionally, for 20 minutes. Add the garlic cloves and cumin and cook for another 10 to 20 minutes, stirring frequently, or until the onions are sweet and golden in color. Keep an eye on them at this stage to make sure they don't burn. Set aside to cool completely.

Once the onions have cooled, put the sour cream and mayonnaise in a medium bowl. Using a rubber spatula, mix until smooth. Add the caramelized onions and stir until just combined. Taste, adding salt and pepper as needed, and garnish with chives, if using. Refrigerate for at least 3 hours, preferably overnight, or up to 3 days.

TIP: Add ground turkey and garlic to your leftover onion dip by browning 8 ounces of ground turkey in 2 tablespoons of olive oil, seasoning with ½ teaspoon of onion powder and ½ teaspoon of kosher salt. When the turkey starts to brown but is not fully cooked, add three small, finely minced garlic cloves and continue to brown the turkey, stirring often. Once fully cooked, set aside to cool completely before combining it with about half a recipe of onion dip. Top with a teaspoon or two of finely chopped parsley.

Yield: About 30 pieces

- Flour, for the work surface
- ½ recipe Quick Puff Pastry (page 26) or store-bought
- 1 package mini sausages (about 30)
- 1 egg
- 2 teaspoons water
- 2 tablespoons small seeds, such as fennel, caraway, poppy, or everything bagel seasoning
- Whole-grain mustard, for serving

My advice? Skip the valet. —Lorelai

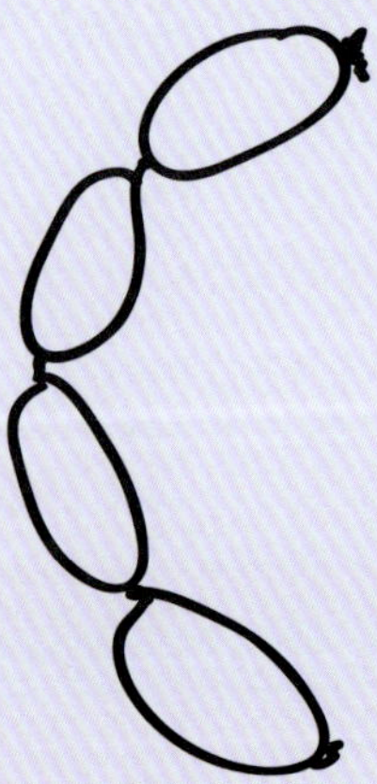

Mini "Bratwursts"

Mini franks in puff pastry are pigs in a blanket—get outta here with that regular old, ordinary, peasant party food! Mini bratwursts, however? Now you're talking! Definitely more sophisticated than your garden-variety-gazeBLAH standard.

One bite of these and you'll be digging up your best sweater vest, jury-rigging your bedroom with plausible body doubles, and hunting down the nearest neighborhood parade so you can serenade your city with "Danke Schoen" as you float your way down Main Street surrounded by lederhosen-laden backup dancers harmonizing to your every note. And praying you don't get caught playing hooky from school. (If you don't get that classic '80s movie reference, you'll have to answer to Lorelai.)

Prepare these sausages using my scratch Quick Puff Pastry (page 26), an organic, nitrate-free sausage (if it's available), and a whole-grain mustard for dipping.

Prepare two baking sheets with silicone baking mats or parchment paper.

On a lightly floured surface, roll out the puff pastry into about an 8-by-11-inch rectangle. Using a pastry wheel or paring knife, cut the pastry into strips about 1½ by 3 inches. Wrap each strip around the center of each sausage (the ends will be exposed) and press to seal. Place the wrapped sausages, seal-side down, on one of the prepared baking sheets. Repeat until all the sausages are wrapped.

Refrigerate for at least 15 minutes before baking. When ready to bake, preheat the oven to 400°F and whisk the egg and water in a small bowl to create an egg wash. Brush the puff pastry with the egg wash and sprinkle with your seeds of choice. Bake for 15 to 20 minutes or until the pastry is golden brown and flaky. Serve with whole-grain mustard.

TIP: These sausages can be prepared ahead without egg wash or topping and frozen for emergency appetizer needs. Place the pastry-wrapped sausages on baking sheets and put them in the freezer for 20 to 30 minutes until very firm. Then store them in an airtight container and freeze until needed or up to 1 month. When ready to bake, preheat the oven and follow the directions above, adding 3 to 5 minutes of extra baking time.

Bracebridge Dinner Butternut Squash Soup

Maybe I can't smell an incoming snowfall on the air, but believe me, I bring my own talents to the table. Usually literally, because my skills are mostly of or related to the kitchen arena, obviously—and making use of fresh, seasonal ingredients. Some say I'm known as the second-best chef of our lifetime. After Alain Ducasse. (Yep, second-best. Second. Like that's a compliment!)

Much like Paul Anka the dog will never forget his first "sugar toe," I'll carry the memory of Christopher saying that to my grave. To the afterlife. To my next life! Well, I'm sorry, but Mr. Christopher Planetarium never tasted this soup. Fresh, roasted butternut squash is blended velvety-smooth with crème-fraîche and finished with an aromatic sprig of rosemary. A warm pot of this on the first snow of the season and no one will ever call you a runner-up again (ahem, Christopher).

Yield: About 8 cups (6 servings)
V, V+*, GF

SPECIAL TOOL:

- Immersion blender

- ¼ cups olive oil
- 1 yellow onion, diced
- 1 teaspoon salt
- 1 teaspoon fresh minced rosemary
- 1 butternut squash (about 2 pounds), peeled and cut into large pieces
- 4 to 5 cups vegetable broth
- Crème fraîche, for garnish (optional)
- Coriander olive oil (page 21), for garnish (optional)
- Rosemary sprigs, for garnish (optional)

NOTE: This soup can easily be served vegan by omitting the crème fraîche or replacing it with a plant-based option such as a coconut-based yogurt.

In a Dutch oven over medium-high heat, heat the olive oil. When it begins to shimmer and coats the bottom of the pan, add the onion, salt, and minced rosemary and sauté until the onions are very soft and beginning to brown, 3 to 5 minutes. Add the butternut squash pieces and continue to sauté for 5 to 7 minutes, until the squash is well coated in the oil and onions.

Add 4 cups of the vegetable broth, reserving the remaining 1 cup for use if needed. Bring the mixture to a boil, then reduce the heat to medium-low to simmer. Cover and simmer, stirring occasionally, for 30 to 40 minutes, until the squash is very tender. Remove from the heat and use an immersion blender to purée until completely smooth. If serving immediately, return to the stove over medium-low heat and reheat, stirring frequently. Add the remaining stock as needed to create the desired consistency.

To serve, ladle into bowls and garnish with a dollop of crème fraîche, a drizzle of oil, and a small sprig of rosemary, if desired.

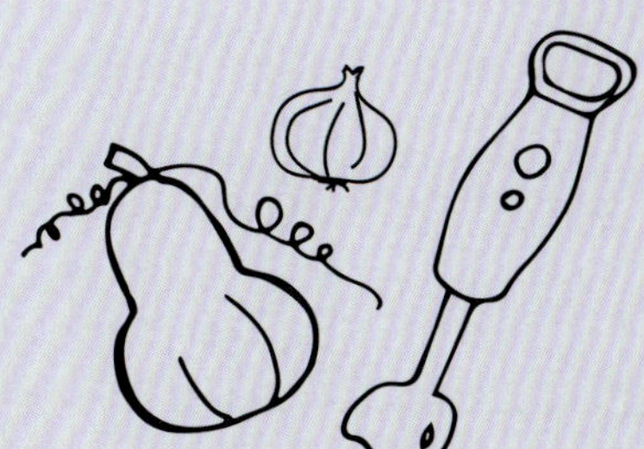

Yield: 16 angel wings; 16 drumettes; 1½ cups dipping sauce
GF*

DIPPING SAUCE:

- ½ cup unseasoned rice wine vinegar
- ¼ cup granulated sugar
- 2 tablespoons packed light brown sugar
- 6 cloves garlic, finely minced (about 1½ teaspoons)
- 1 teaspoon finely minced or grated ginger (about ½-inch piece fresh ginger)
- 1 tablespoon soy sauce or tamari
- ½ cup plus 2 tablespoons water, divided
- 2 to 3 tablespoons sambal oelek
- 1 tablespoon cornstarch

ANGEL WINGS:

- 2 teaspoons minced fresh garlic (about 3 cloves)
- 1 teaspoon fish sauce
- 1 teaspoon soy sauce or tamari
- 2 teaspoons granulated sugar
- 1 teaspoon kosher salt
- 1 tablespoon sesame or vegetable oil
- 16 whole chicken wings (see tips)

Ingredients continue on page 61

NOTE: This recipe can be made gluten free by using tamari or gluten-free soy sauce. The glass noodles should be gluten free, but make sure by checking the label.

Rory's Birthday Angel Wings with Sweet Chile Dipping Sauce

Some parents make their kids' favorite meals for 'em. Like how Luke makes a burger for Lorelai and Rory basically every day. (Usually for breakfast and, okay, he's not their parent, but he's the most stable adult presence in their life. Also, he gives them vegetables.)

Some parents make reservations—that's the Emily Gilmore way. On nights when her cook is off, Emily books a table. Some parents make a phone call to their favorite takeout joint. No judgment (eh . . . a tiny bit of judgment), but Lorelai? I might be looking at you. Sweetie, you know I love you, but your menu drawer is so stuffed it refuses to close. Time to give the Chinese place a rest and try these crispy Thai-inspired angel wings instead! We almost served these at Rory's Sweet 16 party, remember? But you can make 'em any old day of the week. With ground pork, sweet chile dipping sauce for a little kick, and glass noodles for maximum carb-age. You'll be all grown up before you know it.

These wings are totally heaven sent, pun fully intended.

TO MAKE THE DIPPING SAUCE: In a small saucepan over medium-high heat, bring the vinegar, granulated sugar, brown sugar, garlic, ginger, soy sauce, and ½ cup of the water to a boil, stirring until the sugar dissolves. Allow it to boil for 2 minutes. Stir in 1 tablespoon of the sambal oelek at a time, tasting and adding more to reach the desired spiciness. Boil until the sauce begins to thicken and the garlic softens, 3 to 5 minutes.

Meanwhile, in a small bowl, combine the cornstarch and remaining 2 tablespoons of water and stir until smooth. Add the cornstarch slurry to the sauce, reduce the heat to medium-low, and simmer for 2 minutes, or until the sauce thickens. Set the sauce aside to cool before transferring to a glass container with an airtight lid; refrigerate for up to 1 week.

TO MAKE THE ANGEL WINGS: In a medium bowl, combine the garlic, fish sauce, soy sauce, sugar, salt, and sesame oil, stirring to blend.

Using kitchen shears or a sharp knife, separate the flat wing from the drumette at the joint. Add the drumettes to the bowl with the marinade.

Twist to break the joint between the wingette and the wing tip. Using kitchen shears, debone the wingettes by snipping the meat from the bone, starting at the opening. Pull the skin down and continue to snip where you find resistance from cartilage or fat, until you are able to twist and remove the two bones attached to the tip. Put the meat into the bowl with the drumettes. Toss well to coat and marinate overnight.

TO MAKE THE FILLING: Heat the oil in a large sauté pan over medium-high heat. Add the mushrooms, reduce the heat to medium, and cook for 5 minutes, stirring regularly. Add the onions and salt, reduce the heat to medium-low, and cook until the onions become translucent and the moisture has cooked out of the vegetables, about 10 minutes. Set aside to cool.

In a medium bowl, soak the glass noodles in room-temperature water for 10 minutes. Drain the noodles in a colander. In the same bowl, combine the pork, scallions, garlic, carrot, fish sauce, and pepper. Using kitchen shears or a sharp knife, cut the glass noodles into ¾-inch pieces and add to the pork mixture. Add the cooled mushroom mixture. Knead together with your hand or a rubber spatula until well mixed. Use the filling mixture immediately or store in an airtight container for up to 2 days.

When ready to stuff, line a baking sheet with parchment paper. Remove the wings from the marinade and pat off any excess liquid with a paper towel. To stuff the wings, tightly pack the boneless cavity with the pork filling, leaving ½ inch of skin at the top. Place one skin flap over the other and, using a toothpick, thread the two sides of skin together across the top to seal in the filling. If you are struggling to pierce the skin with a toothpick, use a sharp paring knife to prick the holes first. Arrange the wings on the prepared baking sheet in a single layer.

Preheat the oven to 425°F.

Bake for 20 minutes. Flip and cook for an additional 10 minutes, or until nicely browned. Serve immediately, garnished with cilantro (if using), with the dipping sauce, or allow to cool and refrigerate overnight, stored in an airtight container. Reheat at 350°F for about 15 minutes or until heated through.

Stars Hollow—solar panels?
Email this week.
—Taylor

FILLING:

- 2 tablespoons sesame or vegetable oil
- 2 cups roughly chopped mushrooms
- 1 cup finely diced yellow onion
- 1 teaspoon kosher salt
- 1 ounce glass noodles
- 1 pound ground pork
- 6 scallions, chopped
- 1 tablespoon finely minced garlic (about 3 cloves)
- ½ cup shredded carrot
- 1 tablespoon fish sauce
- 2 teaspoons white or black pepper
- 10 sprigs cilantro, for garnish (optional)

TIPS: Ask your butcher to pretty please debone the wingettes (or "flats"—you get bonus insider points for phrasing), keeping the tips attached. No sous-chef? No problem!

You will need wingettes with the wing tips still attached. The drumettes can be either marinated and cooked alongside the angel wings for another delicious element or saved for another use.

Yield: 6 to 8 servings
GF

Brie Wheel with Lavender Honey and Bourbon-Candied Pecans

Kids love wheels! Right? Think about it: The song about buses having wheels . . . That book with the little train engine that could . . . (Wait—do trains have wheels? Something has to move the train over the tracks, right? What do I look like, some kind of train expert? I'm a chef!)

But wheels are always fun . . . So, kids love wheels. And kids love cheese. And objectively, it goes without saying that Brie is the best cheese for starters and cheese plates—spreadable, creamy, and yummy . . . Given all those very true and inarguable facts, it makes total sense that I served this to a wizards-and-elves-and-magical-jewelry-themed child's birthday party. Picky party guests? More of the precious for you.

BOURBON-CANDIED PECANS:

- 1 cup raw pecan halves
- 2 tablespoons unsalted butter
- ½ teaspoon salt
- 1 tablespoon granulated sugar
- ¼ cup bourbon

BRIE:

- One 18-ounce Brie wheel
- ¼ cup honey
- 1 teaspoon dried culinary lavender or herbs de Provence
- Lavender blossoms, for garnish (optional)
- Sliced baguette or crackers, for serving

TO MAKE THE BOURBON-CANDIED PECANS: Line a baking sheet with parchment paper and preheat the oven to 300°F.

In a medium skillet over medium-high heat, toast the pecans and stir frequently until they become fragrant, 2 to 3 minutes. Reduce the heat to medium, add the butter, and as it begins to foam, add the salt and sugar. Stir to coat the pecans. Shake out into a single layer and cook until the sugar dissolves and the mixture begins to brown, 5 to 7 minutes. Stir occasionally and then return the nuts to a single layer.

Carefully add the bourbon. Once the bubbles and steam die down, deglaze the pan, scraping it with a spoon to loosen any flavorful bits. Increase the heat to medium-high and simmer until the liquid is almost gone and the mixture is syrupy, 3 to 5 minutes. Remove the pan from the heat, place the nuts in a single layer on the prepared baking sheet, and bake for 3 to 5 minutes until dry. Allow to cool and then store in an airtight container.

TO MAKE THE BRIE: With the Brie cold from the refrigerator, cut the rind off the bottom of the wheel. Then, working with the exposed cheese facing up, cut the Brie across, working from side to side, making the cuts about 1 inch apart. The cuts should go almost all the way through but not cut through the remaining rind. Rotate the wheel and make the same cuts again, creating cubes. Place the Brie on a serving plate and set aside (see note).

When ready to serve, combine the honey and culinary lavender in a small saucepan over medium heat and bring to a boil. Simmer for 1 to 2 minutes. Pour the hot honey over the Brie. Arrange the pecans on the top and garnish with lavender blossoms, if using. Serve immediately with baguette slices or let rest at room temperature for up to 30 minutes before serving if the cheese is too hard to spread.

Call me for my vegan alternative.
—Mrs. Kim

My mother makes vegan Brie now.
—Lane

NOTE: Brie should soften and come to room temperature for about 30 minutes before serving.

Perfect for
a kid's bday
party!

Yield: 30 to 36 pieces
GF*

- 1½ cups walnuts
- 2 tablespoons honey
- 1 tablespoon water
- ¼ teaspoon ground nutmeg
- 6 ounces Gorgonzola cheese
- ½ cup (8 tablespoons) unsalted butter, softened
- ½ teaspoon kosher salt
- Freshly ground black pepper
- 1 baguette, thinly sliced
- 1 cup baby arugula
- 2 teaspoons olive oil
- Pinch of sea salt or other finishing salt

NOTE: This recipe is easily made gluten free by using a gluten-free baguette.

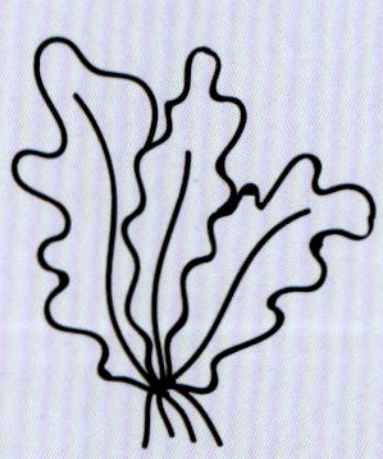

Walnut Arugula Gorgonzola Crostini

Here in Stars Hollow, we cater to our pets' high standards. Often literally.
(I mentioned Paul Anka's love of a good "sugar toe," didn't I?) And the rest of us? The rest of us will eventually find ourselves at a funeral (or similar) for someone else's four-legged friend. That's if we're not catering it ourselves.

I'm thri-xcited (thrilled + excited) to tell you that Michel (!) deemed these crostini sophisticated enough for Chin-Chin the chow's funeral. Arugula, lettuce's peppery, spicy, mature older cousin, is in town for the weekend, showing you the cool vintage spots to shop. Walnuts for crunch. Chin-Chin would have panted in our general direction.

Cover two baking sheets with silicone baking mats or parchment paper.

Put a large skillet over high heat for 1 minute. Toast the walnuts and stir constantly for 1 minute. Remove the pan from the heat and continue to stir occasionally until the walnuts are fragrant and toasted, 2 to 3 minutes.

Pour the walnuts out onto a large plate or baking sheet to cool. Return ½ cup of the walnuts back to the pan over medium-high heat and add the honey, water, and nutmeg. Stir until well combined and bring to a boil. Stir frequently until most of the liquid has evaporated, 3 to 5 minutes. Turn out the walnuts in a single layer onto a piece of parchment paper to cool completely.

Put the rest of the walnuts into the bowl of a food processor and pulse a few times. Add the cheese and pulse again. Add the softened butter and process until a paste forms. Add the salt and pepper to taste and pulse again to combine. Spread a thick layer of this spread onto each baguette slice and place on the prepared baking sheets. Repeat until all the bread has been covered. Freeze the baking sheets for at least 15 minutes.

When ready to bake, preheat the oven to 375°F. Bake the crostini for 12 to 15 minutes or until golden brown and crispy.

While the crostini are baking, in a medium bowl, lightly dress the arugula with the olive oil and sea salt. To serve, place a few arugula leaves and one or two pieces of candied walnuts onto each crostini and serve immediately. Leftover spread can be stored in the refrigerator in an airtight container for up to 3 days and used to make more crostini. Frozen, assembled crostini can be stored in an airtight container or bag in the freezer for up to 1 month.

Mourning Mock Turtle Soup

Turtleneck soup. Richard asked for this one after his mother died. Her "turtleneck soup" was his favorite dish from childhood. Once I guessed what he meant, I whipped up this comforting spin on a traditional mock turtle soup. Try different types of ground meat for different moods. (Turtlenecks optional. Tambourines always a plus.)

Yield: 6 to 8 servings

- 3 tablespoons salted butter
- 1½ pounds lean ground sirloin
- 1 teaspoon kosher salt, plus more as needed
- 1 cup chopped yellow onion (about 1 onion)
- 3 cloves garlic, minced
- 2 teaspoons dried oregano
- 1½ cups chopped celery (about 5 large stalks)
- 4 cups beef broth, preferably bone broth, divided
- ¼ cup all-purpose flour
- 3 dried bay leaves
- One 6-ounce can tomato paste
- ¼ cup Worcestershire sauce
- 4 sprigs thyme
- Juice from 1 lemon (about 2 tablespoons)
- ¼ teaspoon black pepper, plus more as needed
- 5 large hard-boiled eggs (see note)
- ¼ cup sherry, plus more as needed
- ½ cup loosely packed fresh parsley leaves

In a large pot or Dutch oven over medium-low heat, melt the butter. Increase the heat to medium and add the ground sirloin and salt. Cook for about 10 minutes, breaking up the meat with the back of a wooden spoon, until it is well browned. Using a slotted spoon, transfer the meat to a small bowl and set aside. Add the onion, garlic, oregano, and celery to the pot. Increase the heat to medium and sauté until tender but not yet brown, stirring frequently, 5 to 10 minutes. Add the cooked beef.

In a small bowl, whisk ½ cup of the beef broth with the flour. Stir the flour mixture into the meat mixture. Cook over medium-high heat for 1 minute until the broth has been absorbed. Add the remaining 3½ cups of beef broth, the bay leaves, tomato paste, Worcestershire sauce, thyme, and salt to taste. Bring to a boil. Reduce the heat to medium-low, cover, and simmer for 1 hour, stirring occasionally. Add the lemon juice and cook, uncovered, for another 30 minutes, stirring often. Taste and add more salt and pepper as needed. Finely chop three of the five hard-boiled eggs and add to the soup. Quarter lengthwise, or roughly chop, the remaining two eggs and reserve for garnish. Stir in the sherry, adding more if desired. Remove the Dutch oven from the heat. Serve the soup immediately in bowls topped with the egg garnish and parsley leaves. This soup is even better the next day or two.

If making ahead of time, store refrigerated in an airtight container for up to 3 days, adding the sherry, egg wedges, and parsley just before serving.

NOTE: To hard-boil the eggs, place them in a medium saucepan and cover completely with water 1 inch above the eggs. Put the saucepan over high heat and cook until it just reaches a boil. Remove from the heat, cover, and set aside for 10 minutes, setting a timer. Put ice and water into a large bowl. Using a slotted spoon, place the cooked eggs into the ice bath and allow to sit for 10 minutes. Crack the eggs at the base of the shell and peel carefully. They can be made up to 3 days ahead.

Yield: 6 to 8 servings

BACON AND TOMATO CROUTONS:

- 4 small (or 2 large) ripe red tomatoes, finely chopped
- ½ teaspoon salt
- ½ loaf ciabatta bread, cut into ¾-inch cubes
- 2 small or 1 large clove garlic, smashed
- 8 slices thick-cut bacon, cut into 1-inch pieces

Ingredients continue on page 67

"The Lettuce Is Dry" BLT Soup

Knock knock.

Who's there?

Lettuce.

Lettuce who?

Lettuce in, we're freezing out here!

Ba-dump-tss!

Oh, excuse me if they're not all solid gold. Jackson laughed. The truth is: Anything can be a soup if you just believe. Also, if you've already paid for the ingredients and need to find a way to use them up. It's like being on your own personal reality cooking competition show: Clock's ticking, figure it out! Chop chop, literally!

The best part about the whole mix-and-match angle is it means you have options galore: Cold! Hot! Potato! No potato! Chicken stock or vegetarian! Galore! Galore, I say! Don't let dry lettuce get you down. Slap on your best matching skirt suit and strut your stuff in a mother-daughter fashion show, just like Lorelai and Emily back in Rory's Chilton days. Girls just wanna have soup!

TO MAKE THE BACON AND TOMATO CROUTONS: Preheat the oven to 350°F.

Put the tomatoes in a colander over a bowl. Sprinkle the salt over the tomatoes and let sit for 15 minutes. Reserve the strained liquid for the mayonnaise sauce.

On a baking sheet, combine the bread, tomatoes, garlic, and bacon. Bake for 5 minutes and mix the bread well to coat with the tomatoes. Continue to bake for another 30 to 40 minutes, stirring often, or until the tomatoes have thickened, the bread is no longer soggy, and the bacon is crisp. Put the baking sheet on a wire rack to cool.

TO MAKE THE LETTUCE SOUP: Rinse the lettuce leaves well and place standing up in a colander to drain. In a medium saucepan over medium-low heat, cook the butter and onion, stirring often, for 5 to 10 minutes, or until soft. Add the garlic. Sauté for 2 minutes, stirring frequently.

Chop the lettuce. Add the lettuce, chives, and parsley to the saucepan and sauté until wilted, 5 to 7 minutes. Add the lemon juice and broth. Increase the heat to medium-high and bring to a very gentle simmer. Lower the heat to medium-low and continue to cook, uncovered, stirring occasionally, for about 10 minutes. Stir in the crème fraîche. In two batches, transfer the soup to a heat-resistant high-speed blender. Starting on low speed and increasing to high speed, blend until the soup is smooth, 3 to 5 minutes. Add salt and pepper to taste, blending again until smooth. If not serving immediately, cool completely and store in an airtight container, refrigerated, for up to 3 days.

TO MAKE THE MAYONNAISE SAUCE: In a small bowl, combine the mayonnaise, garlic, lemon juice, and tomato juice.

Serve the soup reheated or chilled. Garnish with the croutons, a dollop of mayonnaise sauce, and a pinch of microgreens, if using.

TIP: If you make something a day or two ahead, always taste it again before serving. The flavors develop as the dish sits in the refrigerator, often requiring a bit more salt and pepper.

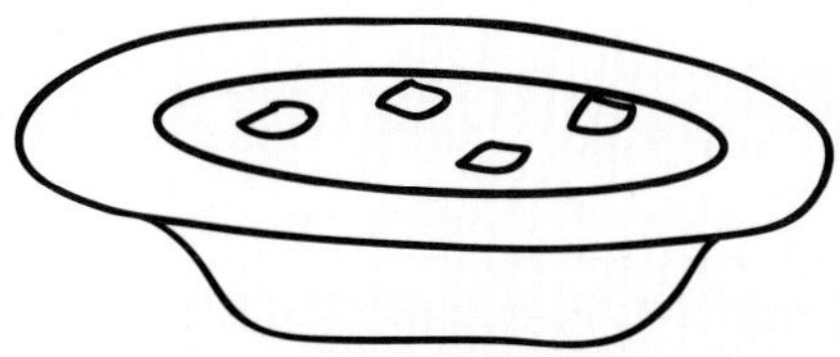

LETTUCE SOUP:

- 1 pound romaine lettuce
- 3 tablespoons salted or unsalted butter
- 1 small yellow onion, chopped
- 3 large cloves garlic, finely minced
- $\frac{1}{3}$ cup coarsely chopped chives, plus more for garnish
- $\frac{1}{2}$ cup coarsely chopped parsley, plus more for garnish
- Juice from 2 lemons (about $\frac{2}{3}$ cup, reserving 1 teaspoon for the mayonnaise sauce)
- 4 cups chicken or vegetable broth
- $\frac{1}{4}$ cup crème fraîche
- Salt
- Freshly ground black pepper
- Microgreens, for garnish (optional)

MAYONNAISE SAUCE:

- $\frac{1}{3}$ cup mayonnaise
- 1 teaspoon minced garlic
- 1 teaspoon lemon juice
- 1 tablespoon juice from salting the tomatoes for the croutons

Yield: 6 to 8 servings
V*, GF*

SPECIAL TOOLS:

- Immersion blender
- Kitchen thermometer

MUSHROOM SOUP:

- 1½ ounces dried shiitake or porcini mushrooms, rinsed well
- 2 cups warm water (about 100°F), plus more as needed
- 3 tablespoons unsalted butter, divided
- 1 medium yellow onion, chopped
- 3 large cloves garlic, minced
- 1 large fennel bulb, chopped, reserving the fronds for garnish if available
- 1 large carrot, chopped
- 1½ pounds fresh mushrooms (shiitake, cremini, and/or button), sliced, divided
- 1¼ teaspoons salt, divided, plus more as needed
- 4 cups beef, chicken, or vegetable broth
- 1 shallot, thinly sliced
- 1½ teaspoons chopped fresh thyme
- Freshly ground black pepper
- ¼ cup sherry or Madeira, plus more as needed (optional)
- 4 ounces crème fraîche

Ingredients continue on page 69

Emily's "This Is Delicious" Mushroom Soup

"This is delicious" is exactly what Emily said the first time she sampled this mushroom soup for a DAR luncheon Lorelai and I were catering. Verbatim. I know—sounds like a compliment. But it was more about the tone—which was kind of . . . surprised?

Yeah, Lorelai's concerns about working for her mom were . . . valid. But the only thing in this world that might talk—even faster than Lorelai—is cold, hard cashola. (It says, "Take the catering job even though your mom's high-maintenance, Lorelai . . . I'm so pretty, Lorelai . . . You're so pretty, Lorelai . . .")

Those stacks of pretty, pretty cash . . . come on! And anyway, Emily did like the soup—even if that seemed to shock her. This is also Jackson's favorite soup. (Because it's delicious!) We rotate the mushroom varieties—experiment with your favorites!—but sherry and thyme are a must.

TO MAKE THE MUSHROOM SOUP: Put the dried mushrooms in a small bowl. Cover with the warm water and set aside for 30 minutes. Using tongs or a slotted spoon, remove the mushrooms from the liquid, slice if whole, and set aside.

In a large heavy-bottomed stockpot or Dutch oven over medium-low heat, melt 2 tablespoons of the butter. Add the onion, garlic, fennel, and carrot and sauté, stirring, for about 10 minutes, or until the vegetables are soft but not yet browned. Increase the heat to medium and add 1 pound of the fresh mushrooms and the rehydrated mushrooms. Cook uncovered for 7 minutes, stirring occasionally. Cover the pan and cook for another 20 minutes. Add 1 teaspoon of the salt.

Add the broth and bring to a simmer. Reduce the heat to low, cover, and cook for 20 minutes. Meanwhile, melt the remaining 1 tablespoon of butter in a medium skillet over medium-low heat. Add the shallot, reserved ½ pound of fresh mushrooms, and the thyme. Add the remaining ¼ teaspoon of salt. Cover and cook for 10 minutes, or until the mushrooms release their liquid. Uncover and cook until the liquid has evaporated and the mushrooms are deeply brown.

Turn off the heat. Using an immersion blender, blend until smooth. Add pepper to taste. (Alternatively, cool the soup for an hour or overnight in the refrigerator, and use a high-speed blender.) Reheat to serve or store in an airtight container in the refrigerator for up to 3 days.

TO MAKE THE BRIOCHE CROUTONS: Preheat the oven to 350°F. Line a baking sheet with parchment paper.

Put the brioche cubes in a medium bowl. Add the butter, garlic, and salt. Using a rubber spatula, toss gently until well distributed. Place the cubes on the prepared baking sheet. Bake for 8 to 10 minutes, or until golden brown. Remove from the oven and set aside to cool for 30 minutes. Store in an airtight container at room temperature for up to 5 days. To re-crisp the croutons before serving, place them in a 350°F oven for 3 minutes.

To serve, reheat the soup as needed. Stir in the sherry to taste, if using, or offer on the side. Serve in bowls with a tablespoon-size dollop of crème fraîche in the center and garnish with the sautéed mushrooms. Finish with the croutons and a bit of fennel fronds if available.

BRIOCHE CROUTONS:

- 4 slices Homemade Brioche Bread (page 10), cut ¾ to 1 inch thick
- ½ cup (8 tablespoons) salted or unsalted butter, melted
- 1 clove garlic, minced
- ¼ teaspoon salt

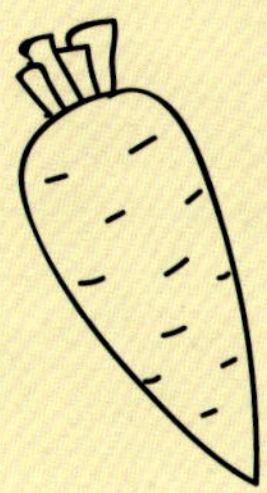

NOTES: This recipe can easily be made vegetarian by choosing a vegetable broth.

If you wish to keep it gluten free, skip the croutons or choose a gluten-free bread alternative.

Chapter Four: Sandwiches, Salads & Sides

Yield: 4 servings
V, V+, GF

- 1 small red beet
- 1 small yellow beet
- 1 small Chioggia beet (see note)
- 2 purple carrots
- 1 small watermelon radish (see note)
- ½ bulb fennel
- 4 ounces snap peas, halved lengthwise
- 8 to 10 small cherry tomatoes, halved
- ¼ cup Lemon-Chive Vinaigrette (page 27)
- Pinch of Maldon or other flaky salt
- Freshly ground black pepper
- Microgreens or baby arugula, for garnish (optional)

NOTE: This is a dish meant for as many colored root vegetables as you can find in the season you find yourself making it, so use what you like and what's available to you. The thinner you cut the slices, the more delicate the taste will be.

Jackson's Vegetables Carpaccio

Sometimes it's too hot to even think about turning the oven on. Some days, you want to keep it light and refreshing. Carpaccio, crudo, tartar, sushi, ceviche . . . All just fancy ways of saying "raw."

Plain and pretty: a plate of bright, colorful vegetables. Color coming out the yin-yang, as Babette might say. So simple, it might blow your mind. (Especially if you're the kind of person who counts the lettuce on your burger as a serving of veggies.)

I came up with this particular presentation when the Dragonfly was down one oven after a(nother?!) fire. I'd wanted to open our kitchen to cooking lessons. Instead, I had to get extra creative. Does that make this dish less Technicolor bright and inviting? No way, José.*

* José = Kirk wearing a name tag Lulu made, just for the purposes of this recipe intro.
If you see him around, say, "Hola, José/Kirk!"

Wash and peel the beets, carrots, and radish. Using a mandoline or the slicing blade on a food processor, slice the beets, carrots, radish, and fennel into very thin slices, keeping them in separate stacks. Arrange the beets, carrots, radish, fennel, snap peas, and cherry tomatoes on individual plates or a platter. Drizzle evenly with the vinaigrette. Cover with plastic and refrigerate for at least 1 hour, or up to 6 hours.

Before serving, sprinkle with the salt. Grind pepper to taste over the vegetables and garnish with microgreens, if using.

Not Jackson's Vegetables Ratatouille

Yield: 8 servings
V, V+, GF

Yes, I should have known better. I agree, I should have left well enough alone. I know, I know—we learned a valuable lesson from the strawberry debacle. I am well aware.

It took ages to rebuild trust after that time Jackson caught me shopping another vendor's fruit stall. If he said the strawberries were no good, I should have believed him . . . But I just couldn't stop myself. It was a horrible betrayal, and I promised I'd never do it again. And I didn't . . . Until I was gifted a sample basket of vegetables from a new vendor and had to decide what to do with them. I tried to resist, but letting them go to waste? I couldn't.

We don't take our frustrations out on the eggs, and we don't let our personal relationships interfere with our professional duty. It's the chef's code. Ratatouille it was, then. And ratatouille it is, here! For you! Roasting the vegetables before combining on the stove brings the flavors alive. It's not cheating if the veggies were free. Right?

- About ½ cup olive oil, divided
- 1 large (or 2 medium) eggplant
- 2 zucchini
- 2 yellow squash
- 2 teaspoons kosher salt, divided
- Freshly ground black pepper
- 1 red bell pepper
- 1 orange bell pepper
- 1 yellow bell pepper
- 1 large (or 2 small) yellow onion
- 5 large cloves garlic, sliced
- 1½ pounds cherry tomatoes
- Fresh basil, for garnish (optional)

Place one oven rack on the top third of the oven and another on the bottom third. Preheat the oven to 400°F. Line two baking sheets with parchment paper and drizzle 1 tablespoon of the oil on each tray.

Using a vegetable peeler, peel zebra stripes lengthwise down the eggplant, alternating flesh and skin. Cut the eggplant into ½-inch cubes and put them into a medium mixing bowl. Toss with 2 tablespoons of olive oil and put the coated eggplant pieces on one of the prepared trays. Cut the zucchini and the yellow squash into ½-inch chunks.

Using the same bowl, toss the zucchini and yellow squash with 1 tablespoon of olive oil and put the coated pieces on the other tray. Shake each baking sheet to distribute the vegetables evenly. Sprinkle ½ teaspoon of salt over each tray. Add some pepper to taste.

Using the two racks in your oven, bake the trays for 30 to 40 minutes, tossing once or twice while rotating the baking sheets every 15 minutes, or until the vegetables begin to caramelize but keep their color. Once cooled, transfer the cooked eggplant, zucchini, and squash to a large serving bowl or platter, keeping the parchment paper on the baking sheets to reuse for the remaining vegetables.

Once the first batch of vegetables has come out of the oven and are cooling, cut the red, orange, and yellow bell peppers into about ½-inch squares. Again, using the same bowl as for the earlier vegetables, toss with 1 tablespoon of olive oil.

Transfer the cut peppers to one of the prepared baking sheets. Cut the onion into 1-inch pieces, put them in the bowl, toss with the garlic and 1 tablespoon of olive oil, and put them on half of the second baking sheet. Last, toss the uncut cherry tomatoes in the bowl with 1½ teaspoons of olive oil and arrange on the other half of the baking sheet with the onions. Sprinkle the remaining 1 teaspoon of salt evenly over all the vegetables on the baking sheets. Add some pepper to taste. Shake the baking sheets to distribute the vegetables evenly. Bake the trays for 30 to 40 minutes, tossing once or twice to ensure even cooking while rotating the baking sheets every 15 minutes, or until the vegetables begin to caramelize but keep their color. Set aside to cool completely.

Combine or arrange the cooled vegetables on the serving platter or bowl. Garnish with basil, if using. The vegetables can be stored separately or combined in airtight containers, refrigerated, for up to 2 days, returning to room temperature before serving.

Trout Salad with Lemon-Chive Vinaigrette

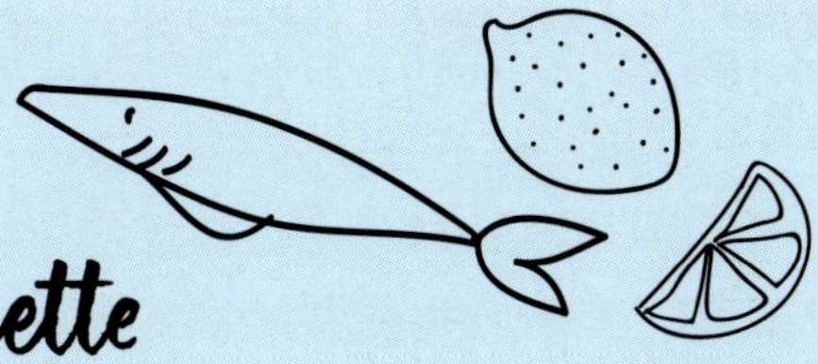

This salad is a refreshing, elegant main course we served at the Bracebridge Dinner. It also makes a great option if you're putting on your own Bracebridge-style event, and you know you'll want choices, especially for those who aren't so jazzed by Bracebridge Dinner Peacock Pie (page 111). (Don't get me wrong—if it were up to me, those people wouldn't be on the guest list in the first place, but what do I know?)

And bonus points to the chef (that's you!) for using the Lemon-Chive Vinaigrette (page 27) and combining two great recipes into one amaze-tastic super-recipe. Go wild! Express yourself! Salad greens, chive blossoms, radish roses, and capers make for a gorj presentation. (You know how I love a good radish rose. But be careful with the paring knife.)

Emily Gilmore insists trout is one of the less-fishy fish, and I concur! Maybe you could even mix some leftovers—if there are any—into the scrambled egg skillet . . . Lane?

Yield: 4 servings
GF

- 6 ounces butter lettuce, red leaf lettuce, or spring mix
- 1 cup pickled cucumbers (see page 22) or sliced fresh
- ¼ cup thinly sliced red onion
- 4 ounces cherry tomatoes
- 8 ounces smoked trout or hot-smoked salmon, broken into bite-size pieces
- ½ cup Lemon-Chive Vinaigrette (page 27)
- 8 Pickled Radish Roses (page 22), for garnish (optional)
- Microgreens, pea shoots, or chive blossoms, for garnish (optional)

Rinse the lettuce and dry well. On a platter or individual plates, arrange the lettuce, pickled cucumbers, red onion, and cherry tomatoes. Top with the smoked trout and drizzle evenly with the vinaigrette.

Garnish with radish roses, microgreens, pea shoots, or chive blossoms, if using.

Yield: 4 to 6 servings
V, V+, GF

- 24 ounces ripe tomatoes, assorted colors if available
- ¼ cup extra-virgin olive oil
- 1 clove garlic, crushed
- ⅛ teaspoon granulated sugar
- 1 teaspoon kosher salt
- Freshly ground black pepper
- 1 tablespoon balsamic glaze
- ¼ cup fresh basil, whole leaves or julienned

Hothouse Tomato Salad with Fresh Herbs

A Sookie signature, my tomato salad earned its place in the New England culinary scene. It's not braggy if it's the truth. Which it is. And not just according to me. *Four Star Dining Magazine* called it a "must-try," and it was a favorite at the Independence.

Once Jackson perfected conditions in his hothouse, we realized not only were our tomatoes the best on the Eastern seaboard—but also—now he grows them year-round! (Take *that*, Jersey tomatoes. Ha ha!)

The only thing to do was to come up with a salad that honored the fruit in all its perfect tomatoey glory. This one is it. Use the tastiest tomatoes you can find—heirloom, beefsteak, cherry, or plum! Top it with a dash of oregano, a drizzle of balsamic vinaigrette, and fresh basil garnish, and forget everything you thought you knew about produce. To-MAY-toe, To-MAH-toe . . . Too good to be true! (But it *is* true!)

Slice the tomatoes and arrange on your serving plates or platter. If you are using cherry tomatoes, cut them in half and add them on top of the sliced tomatoes. In a small bowl, combine the olive oil, garlic, sugar, salt, and pepper to taste and use a spoon to mix well. Drizzle the oil mixture over the tomatoes, then drizzle with the balsamic glaze. Garnish with the basil and serve.

MMMMM
juicy little
tommy-toes!

Roasted Asparagus with Tomatoes and Parmesan Cheese

When I was little, I read a book where the main character called tomatoes "tommy-toes" and it was the cutest. The character was eight. But I still borrow that bit when I'm feeling sassy. You can, too! (Just be warned—people might not find it as cute and charming as, say, your husband does.)

This recipe was developed for the (doomed) launch party Emily Gilmore planned when Richard opened his solo practice with Digger Stiles. (Is it a solo practice when there are two of them? Well, you get the point.)

Handy tip: If you offer this dish to someone named Lorelai—just for example—and they're not into veggies? Try pointing out that it's kinda like a pizza, just if you sub in asparagus for crust and lose the mozzarella. What? It is! Cheese, tomatoes . . . All roasty and oven fresh. (Yeah . . . she didn't go for it, either.)

Yield: 4 or 5 servings
V*, GF

- 1 bunch thin asparagus, trimmed
- 1 tablespoon extra-virgin olive oil
- 2 small cloves garlic, thinly sliced
- ¼ teaspoon salt
- 4 ounces cherry tomatoes, all one color or mixed, halved
- ¼ teaspoon freshly ground black pepper
- Shaved Parmesan cheese, for garnish

Preheat the oven to 425°F.

Put the asparagus on a rimmed baking sheet. Drizzle with the olive oil and toss until evenly coated. Sprinkle evenly with the garlic and salt. Distribute the tomatoes over the asparagus.

Bake for 12 to 15 minutes, or until tender and just turning golden brown. Remove from the oven and set the baking sheet on a wire rack to cool for 5 minutes, or up to an hour if serving at room temperature. Transfer the vegetables to a platter, add a few grinds of fresh pepper to taste, and garnish with the shaved Parmesan.

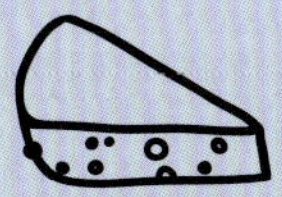

NOTE: This recipe is vegetarian if using vegetarian Parmesan cheese.

Yield: 6 to 8 servings
GF

- 2 cups cherry tomatoes, halved
- 4 cloves garlic, thinly sliced
- ½ teaspoon granulated sugar
- 3 tablespoons extra-virgin olive oil
- ⅛ teaspoon salt
- 12 fresh figs, halved
- 8 ounces burrata cheese
- 8 slices prosciutto
- 1 cup fresh basil leaves
- 2 tablespoons balsamic glaze
- About ⅛ teaspoon Maldon or flaky salt (optional)

Late-Summer Salads: Fig, Prosciutto, and Burrata Salad

Dear Jackson,

Just so you know—a baptism is "just like a bath" the same way burrata is "just like bagged shredded mozzarella from Doose's." *Please*. That's an insult to processed cheese everywhere. A bath involves lit candles, warm water, maybe a gossip magazine to flip through. (Pop stars behaving badly? Yes, please!) When I take a bath, there's no one standing around praying.

If you *really* think there's no difference at all between a religious ceremony and a bath, let's go all-out. Hey—why not just serve this salad in my special favorite fancy bowl that I brought back all the way from Belgium? (Oh wait—you can't, because your family and friends *deep-fried it* on Thanksgiving!)

This sublime salad uses roasted tomatoes, basil, and a balsamic glaze, and I had high hopes it would reunite Lorelai and Rory at the kids' baptism. (It did not.)

Preheat the oven to 325°F. Line a baking sheet with foil.

Put the tomatoes, garlic, sugar, olive oil, and salt on the prepared baking sheet. Toss gently. Roast the tomatoes for 40 to 50 minutes, tossing two or three times, or until golden brown and very tender. Allow it to cool completely.

Just before serving, arrange the figs on a platter. Using your hands, rip the burrata in half, then rip into smaller pieces, arranging them between the figs. Distribute the tomatoes evenly on top. Rip or cut the prosciutto into small pieces and distribute evenly, tucking them decoratively. Garnish with the basil leaves and drizzle with the balsamic glaze. Finish with the flaky salt, if using, and serve immediately.

Late-Summer Salads: Watermelon, Peach, and Feta with Mint Salad

Here's another summer salad from my "baptism, not a bath" days. Even without a post-church luncheon to host, I'm always looking for creative, fresh ways to showcase late-summer fruits and vegetables, and this salad ticks all the boxes. Drizzle with Lemon-Chive Vinaigrette (page 27), dot with your reserved pickled blackberries (see page 18), if you saved them, and serve it up on a bed of greens. (You know greens, Lorelai—sometimes used as garnish? The lettuce on your sandwich you always pick off? Rory carried some in her pocket at that DAR thingy that one time?)

This salad is also more proof that we don't need anything fancy like ovens or stoves to make an amazing meal (although I really didn't need any more proof). Have fun with this one, but if Jackson's cousin Beau wants to add his own special herbs? You say no thank you. PS: Jackson and I are so, so sorry. But not for this salad.

Yield: 6 servings
GF

- 8 ounces baby arugula
- 3 cups seedless watermelon, cut into 1-inch cubes
- 4 peaches, pitted and sliced
- ½ cup crumbled feta
- ¼ cup thinly sliced red onion
- ¼ cup Lemon-Chive Vinaigrette (page 27)
- Freshly ground black pepper
- ¼ cup fresh mint leaves, whole or julienned
- ½ cup pickled blackberries (see page 18) (optional)

Create a bed of arugula on a serving platter. Arrange the watermelon and peaches on top of the arugula. Sprinkle the feta and then the red onion over the fruit. Drizzle with the vinaigrette. Grind fresh pepper evenly over the salad and garnish with the mint and pickled blackberries, if using. Serve immediately.

Yield: 6 to 8 servings
V, V+, GF*

- 5 ounces mixed baby lettuce greens
- 3 cups cooked couscous, cooled (see notes)
- 2 purple carrots (see notes)
- 1 cucumber, peeled and seeded
- 4 sweet peppers (yellow and/or orange)
- 3 scallions, white and light green parts only, thinly sliced
- 1 cup cherry tomatoes, halved
- ¾ cup pink peppercorn oil (see page 21) or good-quality olive oil
- Juice from 1 Meyer lemon (about ¼ cup)
- 2 tablespoons Meyer Lemon–Infused Vinegar (page 19) or champagne vinegar
- ½ teaspoon salt
- 1 teaspoon sumac

Couscous Salad with Garden Vegetables

Couscous—another favorite word to say, and a favorite ingredient to prepare! I love to use it as the base for a cold salad—you could totally serve it as a side, but with the right mix-ins, it's for sure hearty enough to star as a main course. Here I've given you suggestions for some of my favorite veggies to add in. (Don't forget that slicing and dicing are completely different motions and I can hear it in the chop, so don't even try to pull one over on me. Or on yourself. You're only hurting the salad, and what did that delightful couscous ever do to you?)

But back to the salad. You could serve this on a bed of greens. You should play with texture and crunch—walnuts or pepitas would work well in this dish. This salad pairs perfectly with whatever you'd wear to a baptism. (And yes, that outfit you've got on goes great with a baby, too.)

Put the mixed greens in a large low serving bowl or salad bowl and set aside.

Put the couscous in a large mixing bowl. Cut the carrots into thin disks and add to the couscous. Cut the cucumber into half-moons and add to the bowl. Cut the stem off each pepper, use your fingers or a spoon to pull out the core, slice into rings, and add to the bowl. Add the scallions and cherry tomatoes. Set aside.

In a medium measuring cup or bowl, combine the oil, lemon juice, vinegar, salt, and sumac. Whisk until emulsified and add to the couscous bowl. Gently toss until the vegetables are evenly distributed and everything is coated in the dressing.

Place on top of the salad greens and serve.

NOTES: It takes about 1½ cups of dried couscous to make 3 cups.

This recipe can work with many grains, including wild rice, farro, and quinoa, and is gluten free by choosing a gluten-free grain.

Purple carrots are sweet and add gorgeous color, but you can substitute your favorite available carrots.

Warm Potato and Chorizo Salad

Mmmm, potatoes. Smooth, buttery, stick-to-your-ribs yum. Mmmm, pork. Do I even need to remind you how I feel about pork products? (Together again!) This combo was a match made in heaven. Kismet. Fate. Like Luke and Lorelai—destined to end up together. I just rushed it along. (If only I had the same power over people's love lives!)

Chorizo is Spanish for "extra delicious spicy sausage." (I mean, I wouldn't swear on a Bible that's an exact translation, but pretty close.) Hopefully, your plan is to consume them, not pretend to pull them from your significant other's stomach like intestines, "real slow and creepy-like," on Halloween. I'm just saying. It's a good gag—but what a waste of very excellent pork.

Yield: 8 servings
GF

- 2 pounds baby potatoes (red, yellow, or mixed)
- 1 tablespoon kosher salt, plus more as needed
- 8 ounces dried chorizo sausage, casing removed
- 2 shallots, thinly sliced
- 3 tablespoons extra-virgin olive oil
- 1 tablespoon sherry vinegar or red wine vinegar
- Freshly ground black pepper
- ¼ cup chopped fresh parsley
- 4 hard-boiled eggs, for garnish (optional)

Put the potatoes and 1 tablespoon of salt in a large pot. Cover completely with water. Bring to a boil over high heat, reduce the heat to medium, and cook, uncovered, until the potatoes can easily be pierced by a toothpick or knife, 8 to 10 minutes. Using a colander, drain well and set aside to cool. Once cool, cut the potatoes into halves or quarters.

Preheat the oven to 375°F.

Cut the chorizo into ½-inch pieces. Put on a baking sheet with the potatoes, shallots, and olive oil. Toss well. Bake for 20 minutes, tossing once or twice, or until the chorizo is crispy and the potatoes have browned. Remove the pan from the oven and drizzle the vinegar over the potatoes. Toss and transfer to a serving bowl or platter. Add more salt and pepper to taste and garnish with the parsley. If using, chop or cut the eggs into wedges, sprinkle with a little salt, and garnish the salad.

Mini Orange-Glazed Biscuit Sandwiches

A tisket, a tasket . . . a biscuit, a basket . . . (I'm a poet! Kind of an uninspired poem, but hey, it rhymes, doesn't it?) Actually, these would be perfect for a Stars Hollow auction picnic basket—something to keep in mind for next year, maybe? I love mixing savory and sweet, and honey and ham go together like . . . well, like the opposite of Rory and Jess at the auction. You shouldn't have gone on the picnic with him, Rory! Deep down, I know you know that!

Anyway, ham is easy to come by—Emily said she was sent four separate hams after Lorelai Gilmore the first passed away. Four consolation hams! I had no idea consolation hams were a thing, but I'll admit it does make me a little more excited for my next funeral. Hmm. Bad karma? I take it back. Fresh orange zest in the biscuits will have you vitamin-see-ing this dish with heart eyes. Orange you glad I included it?

Yield: 30 mini biscuits

SPECIAL TOOL:

- 1½- to 2-inch round biscuit cutter

ORANGE SUGAR:

- ¼ cup granulated sugar
- 1 tablespoon finely grated orange zest (from about 3 oranges)

ORANGE BUTTER:

- ¼ cup orange juice concentrate
- 2 tablespoons unsalted butter

BISCUITS:

- 4 to 4½ cups pastry or all-purpose flour (see notes), divided, plus more for the work surface
- 1½ tablespoons baking powder
- 1 teaspoon baking soda
- 1½ teaspoons kosher salt
- ¼ cup Orange Sugar
- 1 cup (16 tablespoons) unsalted butter, preferably European style, frozen
- 1¼ cups cold buttermilk, plus more as needed
- ¼ cup frozen orange juice concentrate, thawed
- 2 tablespoons finely chopped candied orange peel (optional)
- ¼ cup Orange Butter

Ingredients continue on page 90

TO MAKE THE ORANGE SUGAR: In a small bowl, combine the sugar and the orange zest and set aside.

TO MAKE THE ORANGE BUTTER: In a small microwave-safe bowl, combine the orange juice concentrate and butter, microwave for 30 seconds, stir until smooth, and set aside.

TO MAKE THE BISCUITS: Preheat the oven to 425°F. Line a baking sheet with parchment paper.

Over a large bowl, sift 4 cups of the flour, the baking powder, baking soda, and salt. Whisk in the orange sugar. Using the large holes on a box grater, grate the frozen butter over the flour mixture.

In a small bowl, combine the buttermilk and orange juice concentrate.

Using a rubber spatula, stir the buttermilk mixture into the flour mixture until just combined, being careful not to overwork the dough. If using, add in the candied orange peel. If too dry, add more buttermilk 1 tablespoon at a time as needed, until a soft, sticky dough forms. Refrigerate the dough in the bowl for 10 minutes before continuing.

ASSEMBLY:

- 1 pound thick-cut sliced ham
- 8 slices sharp cheddar, each cut into 4 squares
- ⅓ cup honey mustard

Transfer the dough to a floured surface. Fold the dough in half over itself, using your hands to gently flatten the layers together. If the dough sticks to your hands, sprinkle a little bit of flour over the dough. Repeat five or six times, rotating the dough 90 degrees each time, sprinkling more flour only as needed to prevent sticking to your hands without overworking the dough. Using a floured rolling pin, gently roll out the dough to about 1 inch thick.

Dip the biscuit cutter (see notes) in flour and firmly press downward into the dough, lift up without twisting, and place the biscuit on the prepared baking sheet. Continue cutting out the biscuits as closely together as possible, spacing them out evenly on the prepared baking sheet, 1 to 1½ inches apart. Put the baking sheet with the biscuits into the freezer for 10 minutes (see notes).

Remove from the freezer, brush the tops with the orange butter, and bake for 12 to 15 minutes, or until golden brown (see notes). Allow to cool completely on a wire rack.

TO ASSEMBLE THE SANDWICHES: Cut the ham into squares slightly larger than the biscuits. Use a fork to poke around the middle of each biscuit horizontally and slowly separate in half to create two halves for sandwiches. Count out your ham squares and divide them among the number of biscuits you have. Place the ham on the bottom of each biscuit, and top with a square of cheddar and add a dollop of honey mustard. Place the tops of the biscuits over the mustard. Arrange on a platter and serve.

NOTES: Pastry flour will produce a slightly lighter biscuit because it contains a lower protein content. The size of your biscuits will determine how long to bake them for, so adjust your time a few minutes more or less as needed.

To make ahead, freeze the biscuits for 1 hour on the tray and then transfer them to resealable bags or freezer-safe containers. Brush with the orange butter before baking. Do not defrost before baking but allow for an additional 2 to 3 minutes of cooking time.

Baked Corned Beef Brisket Sandwiches on Rye

Remember when a train derailed just outside the Stars Hollow town limits? What a pickle—literally! That's not just adorable wordplay; the train was carrying crates and crates of—yep, you guessed it—pickles.

Personally, even with my professionally trained chef's palate, I don't know if I would have said that pickles *have* a particular noticeable smell when there's just one hanging out on your plate next to your burger. Well. It turns out, when you have a *trainload* of pickles lying around for days on end . . . You get the idea.

How you feel about the smell depends on how you feel about pickles. But it's not subtle. And there's no covering it up. So, if you can't beat 'em, join 'em. The whole situation called for a salty slab of brisket and a dollop of mustard. Perfection in a deli sandwich. This is also a great way to make a tender corned beef roast. Now, that's how you get back *on track*! Hee-hee. (It actually took the railroad people a few days.)

Yield: 6 sandwiches
GF*

CORNED BEEF:

- 3 pounds beef brisket, flat or point cut (see notes), or chuck roast
- 2 teaspoons kosher salt
- 1 teaspoon mustard powder
- 1 teaspoon freshly ground black pepper
- 1 teaspoon ground cumin
- 1 teaspoon celery salt
- 1 teaspoon fennel seeds
- 8 whole cloves
- 4 large bay leaves
- ½ cup Dijon mustard

SANDWICHES:

- 12 slices rye bread
- ½ cup (8 tablespoons) salted or unsalted butter, at room temperature
- About ½ cup whole-grain or Dijon mustard
- 2 pounds cooked Corned Beef, sliced
- 12 pickle slices (see page 22)
- Microgreens or pea shoots, for serving (optional)

TO MAKE THE CORNED BEEF: Pat the meat dry with paper towels. Sprinkle the salt on all sides and let sit at room temperature for 30 to 60 minutes, or in the refrigerator in an airtight container overnight.

In a small bowl, combine the mustard powder, pepper, cumin, and celery salt. On a cutting board with a chef's knife, or in mortar and pestle, crush the fennel seeds and cloves. Add the spices and, using your hands, crush in the bay leaves. Stir the mustard into the spices and set aside.

Preheat the oven to 300°F.

Place a large piece of foil in a baking dish larger than the meat. Put the meat on the foil. Rub all sides of the meat with the mustard mixture. Bake for 2½ to 3 hours (see notes), or until fork-tender. Allow to rest for 20 minutes before removing the foil and slicing, or cool completely and refrigerate in an airtight container for up to 5 days. Wrap the portion to be used in foil and reheat in a 350°F oven for 20 minutes, allowing it to rest for 10 minutes before slicing.

TO MAKE THE SANDWICHES: Toast the bread slices and allow them to cool for 5 minutes. Spread the butter on six slices of the toasted bread. Spread the mustard over the other slices and set aside. Distribute the corned beef over the buttered bread. Place the pickles on the corned beef, top with the microgreens, if using, and finish with the reserved bread slices, mustard-side down.

NOTES: Bake for 1 hour per pound and check to see if the meat has reached fork-tender. Bake another 15 minutes per pound as needed. The flat section of a brisket is leaner than the more tender, fattier point section, and a matter of preference.

This recipe can be made gluten free by choosing a gluten-free bread.

Yield: 10 to 12 biscuits, or about 30 mini biscuits

SPECIAL TOOLS:

- Meat thermometer
- 1½- to 2½-inch round biscuit cutter

PORK TENDERLOIN:

- 2 pork tenderloins (about 2 pounds)
- 1 teaspoon kosher salt
- ¼ teaspoon black pepper
- ½ teaspoon paprika
- ½ teaspoon onion powder
- ½ teaspoon garlic powder
- ¼ cup Orange Butter (page 89)

Ingredients continue on page 93

Sweet Potato Biscuit Sandwiches

Here's another invention born from "necessity," depending on your attitude toward pet funerals and whimsy. (Of course, if you're anti-whimsy, this is probably not the cookbook for you. And who are you, anyway, some kind of fun-sucking grump? You're probably the kind of person who donates a wad of cash to the Stars Hollow knitathon rather than knitting with the rest of us, thereby eliminating the need for the knitathon to continue, and ruining everyone's fun. Just if I had to guess. Completely random example off the top of my head . . . Christopher.)

I served these sandwiches at Chin-Chin's wake. Some of my finest work, all "wasted" on a pet funeral, I thought—but it's not a waste now that I've shared it with you! This is also another great opportunity to work on your chutney skills. Which means another chance to say CHUTNEY as much as you want. Three cheers for chutney! Six cheers for chutney! The sky's the limit for you and your chutney-based dreams!

TO MAKE THE PORK TENDERLOIN: Preheat the oven to 400°F. Pat the pork dry with paper towels.

In a small bowl, combine the salt, pepper, paprika, onion powder, and garlic powder.

Place each tenderloin in the center of a piece of foil cut 4 inches longer than the tenderloin. Sprinkle the salt mixture over the tenderloin. Brush the orange butter over the top of the seasoning. Wrap each tenderloin with the foil.

Put the pork in the oven (with the sweet potatoes if making the same day) and bake for 25 to 30 minutes, or until the pork reaches 145°F on a meat thermometer. Remove from the oven and allow to rest for 15 minutes. This can be made up to 2 days ahead of serving. Allow it to cool completely before storing the foil-wrapped pork in the refrigerator.

NOTES: Pastry flour will produce a slightly lighter biscuit because it contains a lower protein content. The size of your biscuits will determine how long to bake them for, so adjust your time a few minutes more or less as needed.

To make ahead, freeze the biscuits for 1 hour on the tray and then transfer them to resealable bags or freezer-safe containers. Do not defrost before baking but allow for an additional 2 to 3 minutes of cooking time.

TO MAKE THE SWEET POTATO BISCUITS: Preheat the oven to 400°F. Line a baking sheet with parchment paper.

Pierce the sweet potatoes with a sharp knife or fork in about five places. Put them on the prepared baking sheet and bake (leaving room for the pork if making the same day) for 1 to 1½ hours, or until very soft. Remove from the oven and let cool for 15 to 30 minutes.

When cool enough to handle, peel and mash the sweet potatoes in a medium mixing bowl. Measure out 1½ cups, saving any remaining sweet potato for another use. Allow it to cool completely. This can be made up to 3 days in advance.

Over a large bowl, sift 4 cups of the flour, the baking powder, baking soda, and salt. Whisk in the orange sugar. Using the large holes of a box grater, grate the frozen butter over the flour mixture.

In a medium bowl, whisk the 1½ cups of the cooled, mashed sweet potato with the buttermilk. Using a rubber spatula, fold it into the flour mixture until just combined, being careful not to overwork the dough. If too dry, add more buttermilk 1 tablespoon at a time as needed, until a soft, sticky dough forms. Refrigerate the dough in the bowl for 10 minutes before continuing.

Transfer the dough to a floured surface. Fold the dough in half over itself, using your hands to gently flatten the layers together. If the dough sticks to your hands, sprinkle a little bit of flour over the dough. Repeat five or six times, rotating the dough 90 degrees each time, sprinkling more flour only as needed to prevent sticking to your hands without overworking the dough. Using a floured rolling pin, gently roll out the dough to about 1 inch thick.

Line a second baking sheet with parchment paper. Dip the biscuit cutter (see notes) in flour and firmly press downward into the dough, lift up without twisting, and place the biscuit on the prepared baking sheet. Continue cutting out the biscuits as closely together as possible, spacing them out evenly on the prepared baking sheet, 1½ to 2 inches apart. Put the baking sheet with the biscuits into the freezer for 10 minutes (see notes). Remove from the freezer and bake for 12 to 15 minutes, or until golden brown (see notes). Allow to cool completely on a wire rack.

TO ASSEMBLE THE SANDWICHES: Slice the tenderloins. Cut each biscuit in half horizontally. Butter the bottoms of each biscuit with the softened butter. Distribute the pork over the buttered biscuit bottom. Top the pork with about 1 teaspoon of apple chutney. Top with the other half of the biscuit and serve immediately.

SWEET POTATO BISCUITS:

- 2 medium sweet potatoes
- 4 to 4½ cups pastry or all-purpose flour (see notes), divided, plus more for the work surface
- 1½ tablespoons baking powder
- 1 teaspoon baking soda
- 1½ teaspoons kosher salt
- ¼ cup Orange Sugar (page 89)
- 1 cup (16 tablespoons) unsalted butter, preferably European style, frozen
- 1 cup cold buttermilk, plus more as needed

ASSEMBLY:

- 2 tablespoons butter, preferably European style, softened
- ½ cup Apple Chutney (page 17)

Chapter Five: Mains

Lamb Chops and Sicilian Olive Gremolata

Yield: 3 to 4 servings
GF

Lamb chops are my go-to for an elegant meal that feels a little more modern than your standard roast. They're as quick and versatile as a roast, plus lamb pairs perfectly with rosemary, one of my favorite herbs. Its woodsy aroma will fill your house—light a fire on a blustery autumn evening, pop these suckers in a preheated oven, and see if I'm lying.

Of course I'm not lying. I didn't lie to Jackson about flirting with that Joe Mastoni when I ran into him outside of the Learning Annex, and I'm not lying to you now. Why would I? I've got nothing to hide! I don't flirt with random men on the street! I'm spoken for! Jackson knows that! Well, he especially knows that now, because I made him these lamb chops and came clean about the whole thing. Good thing I used extra garlic; that definitely also helped soften some of the blow. Serve these with the Warm Potato and Chorizo Salad (page 87) to re-create the meal I made for Jackson!

SPECIAL TOOL:

- Meat thermometer

LAMB CHOPS:

- 8 rib rack Frenched lamb ribs (see note)
- 5 cloves garlic, smashed
- 4 tablespoons olive oil, divided
- 1 teaspoon kosher salt
- 1 teaspoon freshly ground black pepper
- 3 sprigs rosemary

GREMOLATA:

- 1 cup chopped flat-leaf parsley
- 3 tablespoons capers, roughly chopped
- 1 or 2 cloves garlic, finely minced (about 1 teaspoon)
- 2 tablespoons Meyer Lemon–Infused Vinegar (page 19)
- 1 cup coarsely chopped Sicilian olives (or other green olives)

NOTE: Frenched lamb chops refers to removing the fat, meat, and cartilage from the bones, making them both more beautiful and creating a built-in handle for eating.

TO MAKE THE LAMB CHOPS: Slice between the lamb ribs, cutting through the bone as needed, to create eight chops. Try to make cuts of equal thicknesses for more even cooking. Pat the chops dry with paper towels.

In a large bowl, combine the garlic, 2 tablespoons of the olive oil, the salt, and pepper. Add the lamb chops and rosemary, tossing until well coated. Cover and refrigerate for at least 4 hours or overnight.

Remove the lamb chops from the refrigerator 30 minutes before cooking. Put a large cast-iron or heavy-bottomed pan over high heat. Add the remaining 2 tablespoons of olive oil and heat for 1 minute. Add the chops in a single layer, in two batches if needed, and sear for 2 to 4 minutes per side, until they reach your preferred doneness. Use a meat thermometer to determine 130°F for medium rare or 140°F for medium. Transfer to a platter, tent with foil, and let rest for 5 minutes (see tip).

TO MAKE THE GREMOLATA: In a medium bowl, combine the parsley, capers, garlic, vinegar, and olives. Serve immediately or transfer to an airtight container and refrigerate for up to 3 days.

TIP: Salting or marinating meat 4 to 24 hours in advance of cooking dissolves the protein strands, which allows the meat to retain moisture as it cooks, making it tastier, more tender, and extra juicy. Allowing the meat to rest for 5 to 10 minutes (or 15 to 20 minutes if making a large roast) after cooking allows the juices to reabsorb and redistribute, ensuring the juice will not run off and dry out the meat as you cut into it.

Pork Chops with Madeira-Poached Pears

Yes, I know. I know what I said, I remember as well as anyone else. It still haunts me: "No more pork." The worst part is, I meant it in the moment, too!

I take it back, baby! Let's never fight again! I love you, pork! You're the Gavin to my Gwen! The Sid to my Nancy! The . . . the . . . Some other pop culture couple that I'm totally blanking on in the moment, but whatever!

Maybe I didn't discover an entirely new type of protein, but this preparation is big-time hooray. Thick-cut chops are topped with poached pears for a play on your pork-chops-and-applesauce. Rekindle your spark! With pork! Pork and Sookie, together again!

Yield: 4 servings with extra pears
GF

SPECIAL TOOLS:

- Meat thermometer
- Two 16-ounce jars or one 32-ounce jar, sterilized (see tip page 13)

PEARS:

- 2 cups water
- 1 cup granulated sugar
- 1 tablespoon pink peppercorns
- 2 whole star anise
- 2 bay leaves
- 4 ripe, firm pears
- 1 cup sweet Madeira wine

Ingredients continue on page 100

TO MAKE THE PEARS: In a medium pot over medium-high heat, cook the water, sugar, peppercorns, star anise, and bay leaves until the sugar is completely dissolved, 7 to 10 minutes. Remove the pan from the heat and set aside.

Peel, quarter, and core each pear, adding the pieces directly to the pot as you go to prevent discoloring.

Once all the pears have been added, return the pot to the stove over medium-high heat until it begins to boil. Reduce the heat to medium-low and simmer for 20 minutes. Add the Madeira and continue to simmer for another 10 minutes or until the pears are just tender.

Remove from the heat and allow to cool to room temperature before storing in an airtight container or large sterilized jar (see page 13). Refrigerate until needed or up to 5 days.

TO MAKE THE PORK CHOPS: Reserve ½ cup of the poaching liquid, strained of any spices, and set aside. In a large airtight container, combine the remaining ½ cup of the poaching liquid, the water, and ½ cup of the salt. Stir until the salt is dissolved. Place the chops in the liquid, making sure they are submerged, and refrigerate for at least 30 minutes or up to 4 hours.

Line a baking sheet with paper towels. Remove the chops from the brine and put on the prepared baking sheet to dry. Preheat the oven to 350°F.

On a large plate, lay out the tapioca starch and mix in the remaining ½ teaspoon of salt and the pepper to taste. Dredge the shallot slices in

PORK CHOPS:

- 1 cup poaching liquid, from pears above
- 4 cups cool water
- ½ cup plus ½ teaspoon kosher salt, divided
- 4 thick, boneless pork chops
- 2 tablespoons tapioca starch
- Freshly ground black pepper
- 1 large shallot, thinly sliced
- 3 tablespoons olive oil
- 2 tablespoons unsalted butter
- 4 to 6 poached pear quarters, sliced, at room temperature

the tapioca, separating them into ribbons as you go. Set aside. Dredge each chop in the remaining tapioca, getting some on both sides.

In a large skillet or sauté pan over medium-high heat, heat the olive oil and butter. When the butter begins to foam, add the shallots and cook, stirring frequently, until they are golden brown, 5 to 7 minutes. Use a slotted spoon to remove them to a plate and set aside.

Remove the chops from the baking sheet, discarding the paper towels and setting the sheet aside. Add the pork chops to the pan, still over medium-high heat, and brown on both sides, for 3 to 5 minutes per side or until a deep golden brown. Transfer the chops from the pan to the baking sheet and continue to cook in the oven until the internal temperature reaches 140°F. Remove from the oven, tent with foil, and let rest for 5 minutes.

While the chops are in the oven, turn the heat on the pan down to medium and deglaze the pan with the remaining ½ cup of poaching liquid, scraping the pan with a spoon to loosen any flavorful bits. Work in all the fond to the sauce. Add the shallots to the pan and continue to stir until the sauce thickens and coats the back of the spoon. Add the sliced pears and cook for 1 to 2 minutes more or until the pears are warmed through.

To serve, ladle some sauce and pears onto four plates or one serving plate, reserving a few slices for garnish, and top with the pork chops. Arrange two or three pear slices on top of each chop. Serve immediately. This dish pairs well with Roasted Asparagus with Tomatoes and Parmesan Cheese (page 81) and/or simple roasted potatoes.

NOTE: The extra poached pears are delicious added to a sandwich.

"Four in Four" Coq au Vin

In vino veritas, or so they say. In wine, there is truth. Coq au vin is Jackson's favorite, so naturally, I made it for him early in our marriage.

And "<u>in chicken with wine</u>," the man hit me with some truth: He wanted us to have four kids. In four years. (Naturally?) It was a <u>lot</u> of truth to process. Just something to keep in mind, depending on whom you're cooking this for. Just be prepared.

Pearl onions, mushrooms, bacon (hooray!), and—of course—red wine. Delicious. And potentially eye-opening. Bon appétit!

TIP: Start 2 days before serving for even tastier results.

Yield: 4 servings
GF*

COQ AU VIN:

- 4 chicken leg quarters, breast quarters, or a combination
- 1 teaspoon kosher salt, plus more as needed
- ¼ teaspoon freshly ground black pepper, plus more as needed
- 2 cups red wine
- ¼ cup brandy
- 4 sprigs thyme
- 3 bay leaves
- 8 ounces thick-cut bacon, cut into ½-inch pieces
- 8 ounces pearl onions, fresh or frozen, peeled (see notes)
- 3 medium carrots, sliced ½ inch thick at an angle
- 8 ounces cremini mushrooms, sliced or quartered
- 5 cloves garlic, minced
- 2 tablespoons olive oil
- ¼ cup tomato paste
- 1 cup chicken or beef bone broth

Ingredients continue on page 103

TO MAKE THE COQ AU VIN: Put the chicken in a large bowl and sprinkle evenly with the salt and pepper. Let sit for 20 minutes. Add the wine, brandy, thyme sprigs, and bay leaves. Toss to evenly distribute. Cover with a lid or plastic wrap and refrigerate for at least 4 or up to 24 hours.

Remove the chicken from the marinade and transfer to a cutting board, setting the marinade aside. Using paper towels, pat the chicken dry.

In a large Dutch oven over medium heat, fry the bacon, stirring often, until browned, about 5 minutes. Using a slotted spoon, remove the bacon to a medium bowl, leaving the bacon fat in the pan. Add the onions to the Dutch oven and sauté until they begin to turn golden brown, about 10 minutes. Using the slotted spoon, remove the onions and add to the bacon. Add the carrots to the Dutch oven and cook until just turning golden brown, about 10 minutes. Remove and add the onions and bacon. Add the mushrooms to the Dutch oven, cover, and cook for 5 minutes. Take the cover off and continue to cook until the liquid has evaporated and they begin to turn golden brown, about 10 minutes. Add the garlic and cook for 3 minutes. Remove and add to the bacon, onions, and carrots.

Increase the heat to medium-high. Add the olive oil and heat for 1 minute. Add the chicken, skin-side down, and cook for about 5 minutes, until nicely browned. Flip the chicken and brown for another 2 to 3 minutes. Transfer the chicken to a plate and set aside. Add the tomato paste and cook for 3 minutes until it begins to caramelize. Pour the reserved marinade into the pan and boil, uncovered, for 10 to 15 minutes, or until reduced by about half, scraping the pan with a wooden spoon to loosen any flavorful bits. Stir in the broth. Add the chicken, bacon, onions, carrots, and mushrooms to the wine mixture.

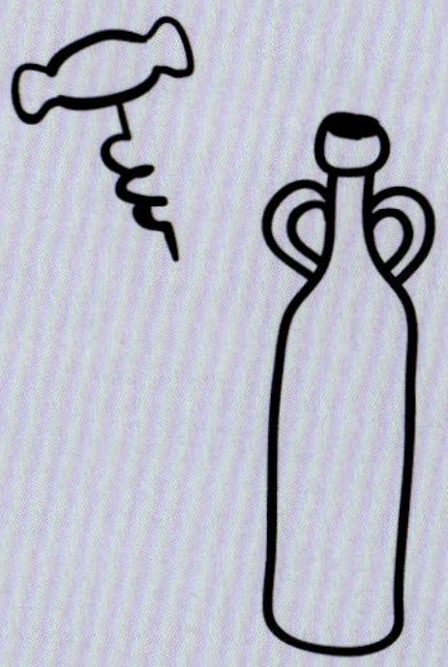

Place a cover on the pot. Reduce the heat to medium and bring to a gentle boil. Reduce the heat to low and simmer slowly for 60 to 90 minutes, until the chicken is tender when pierced with a fork.

TO MAKE THE BEURRE MANIÉ: While the chicken is cooking, in a small bowl, combine the flour with the butter and, using a fork or teaspoon, knead into a smooth paste.

While the coq au vin is hot, or after it has been reheated (reheat in a pot over medium-low heat for 15 to 20 minutes, or until heated through), remove the chicken pieces to a plate. To the sauce in the pot, over medium heat, whisk in one-quarter of the beurre manié at a time, bringing the sauce to a gentle boil and whisking until smooth, until you reach the desired thickness. Add the chicken back to the pan, stir gently, and serve. Refrigerate or freeze any remaining beurre manié for future use thickening soup or gravy.

TIP: Choose a wine you enjoy drinking when using it in your recipes. Bordeaux, Côtes du Rhône, and Cabernet Sauvignon all work well for making a delicious coq au vin and drinking alongside it as well.

BEURRE MANIÉ:

- ¼ cup all-purpose flour (or tapioca starch, for a gluten-free option)
- ¼ cup (4 tablespoons) unsalted butter, softened (or 2 tablespoons, if using tapioca starch)

NOTES: This recipe can be made gluten free by making the beurre manié with tapioca starch.

If you can't find pearl onions, use cocktail onions, rinsing them well before adding them as directed.

Yield: 10 to 12 servings
V*

- 4 cups cubed Homemade Brioche Bread (page 10), French bread, or Italian bread
- ¼ cup (4 tablespoons) salted butter, melted
- 2 cloves garlic, finely minced
- 1½ cups grated Parmesan or pecorino cheese, divided
- 1 tablespoon kosher salt, plus more as needed
- 1 pound dried small elbow, cavatappi, or shell pasta
- 3 cups (two 12-ounce cans) evaporated milk
- 1 teaspoon onion powder
- 1 teaspoon garlic powder
- 2 teaspoons mustard powder
- 4 tablespoons Beurre Manié (page 103)
- ¾ cup (6 ounces) crème fraîche
- 6 ounces Havarti or fontina cheese, grated
- 8 ounces sharp white cheddar cheese, grated
- 6 ounces Gruyère cheese, grated
- Freshly ground black pepper

NOTE: This recipe is vegetarian if using vegetarian Parmesan cheese.

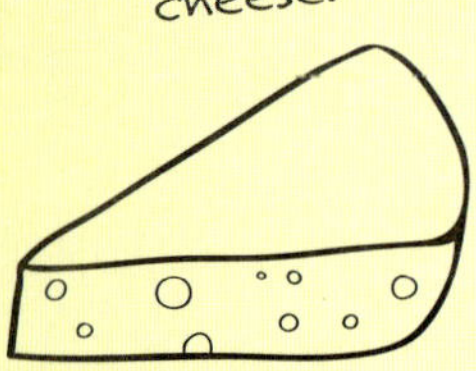

Pasta à la Sookie

This pasta is similar to macaroni and cheese. Like, super-duper similar . . . suspiciously similar . . . Maybe even the exact same thing? Except, unlike the version I served to a birthday party full of children dressed as tiny magical elves with terrible palates, this one isn't green or spicy, so, how about a big crowd-please-y "Yay, Sookie"?!

It turns out the difference between mac and cheese and Pasta à la Sookie is the blend of cheeses you use, the quality of the breadcrumb crust . . . and whether you're serving it to Lorelai and Rory or Emily and Richard. (The more unpronounceable the ingredients, the better. You know you nailed it when Emily says it reminds her of something she once had in Europe.) You won't find a trace of dehydrated orange cheese powder here. And you won't miss it!

Rebranding: priceless. Can I get a "copper boom"!?

Preheat the oven to 350°F.

In a food processor, pulse the cubed bread until it turns into coarse crumbs. Put the breadcrumbs in a medium bowl. Toss with the melted butter and garlic. Put in an 8-by-8-inch baking dish in an even layer. Bake for 10 to 15 minutes, stirring often, or until just turning golden brown. Remove from the oven and toss with ½ cup of the Parmesan cheese. This can be made up to 2 hours in advance before proceeding. Ten minutes before serving, bake for another 3 to 4 minutes, or until golden brown. Set aside.

Fill a large Dutch oven or pot three-quarters full of water and bring to a boil over high heat. Add 1 tablespoon of salt and the pasta. Stir and cook until slightly underdone or just before al dente, about 6 minutes. Reserve 1½ cups of the pasta water. Drain the pasta well and set aside.

In the same pot the pasta was cooked in, whisk the evaporated milk, onion powder, garlic powder, and mustard powder. Whisking constantly, bring the sauce to a simmer over medium heat. Add the beurre manié, 1 tablespoon at a time, whisking constantly. Whisk in the crème fraîche until smooth. Stir in the pasta.

Add half of the Havarti, cheddar, and Gruyère cheeses and stir until combined. Cover, remove from the heat, and let sit for at least 5 or up to 60 minutes. When ready to serve, add ½ cup of the reserved pasta water and reheat over medium heat, stirring constantly. Slowly add the remaining Havarti, cheddar, Gruyère, and Parmesan cheeses. Add more of the pasta water as needed, a little at a time, until you reach the consistency you are happy with. Add salt and pepper to taste. Once the pasta is hot, cover the pot and again let sit for 5 minutes. Stir again, top with the toasted breadcrumbs, and serve.

> *If Sookie is going to put her name on this mac and cheese, you know it will be deliciously rich and creamy.*
>
> *—Lorelai*

TIPS: Cooking pasta in salted water ensures each piece of pasta is evenly seasoned from the inside out by using 1 tablespoon of salt per gallon of water.

Store-bought grated cheese contains anticaking agents that will make your sauce less creamy. Grate it by hand or use the grater blade with your food processor.

Yield: 6 to 8 servings

CASSEROLE:

- ¼ cup plus 2 tablespoons (6 tablespoons total) salted or unsalted butter
- 1 large leek, white part only, well rinsed and chopped
- 3 stalks celery, chopped
- 1 large carrot, chopped
- 3 cloves garlic, minced
- ½ teaspoon salt, plus more as needed
- Freshly ground black pepper
- 4 cups diced rotisserie chicken
- 2½ cups chicken broth
- 1 teaspoon garlic powder
- 1 tablespoon fresh thyme leaves or 1½ teaspoons dried
- ½ cup all-purpose flour
- 1½ cups heavy cream or half-and-half

DROP BISCUITS:

- 1½ cups all-purpose flour
- 1½ teaspoons baking powder
- ¾ teaspoon baking soda
- ½ teaspoon salt
- ⅓ cup (5 tablespoons plus 1 teaspoon) salted butter, frozen, plus 2 tablespoons melted, divided
- ¾ cup buttermilk
- ¼ cup chopped chives
- ¼ cup chopped parsley

Chicken and Dumpling Casserole

A classic with a light drop biscuit crust, this casserole is a great make-ahead dish for potlucks or family gatherings . . . or, for instance, any old Saturday night. Like say, if you've got dinner plans with your husband, your bestie, and her fiancé, and you're not even on the hook for cooking? It's always nice to bring a dish. (Personally, I bring a casserole wherever I go. Weird? Or thoughtful? Or why not both?) Maybe it'll detract from all that awkward arguing about stuff like voicemails from exes and spooky old bedroom sets—or whatever you and yours argue about when you hang out. (Casseroles are very comforting food.)

I know, I know, it's traditional to bring something to accompany the dinner, not a whole second dinner. But people like options, right? If we learned anything from Rory's decision to go to Yale instead of Harvard, it's that people can surprise you!

TO MAKE THE CASSEROLE: Preheat the oven to 350°F. Grease a 9-by-13-inch baking dish with 2 tablespoons of the butter.

In a large skillet over medium-low heat, melt ¼ cup of the butter. Add the leek, celery, carrot, and garlic. Sauté for 8 to 10 minutes, until the vegetables are soft but not yet brown. Add the salt and pepper to taste. Stir in the chicken, chicken broth, garlic powder, and thyme. Increase the heat to medium and stir until just simmering.

Meanwhile, in a small bowl, whisk the flour and cream until smooth. Slowly stream the cream mixture into the chicken mixture. Continue cooking over medium heat until it thickens, resembling partially reconstituted condensed soup, about 5 minutes. Put into the prepared baking dish.

TO MAKE THE DROP BISCUITS: In a large bowl, use a fork to combine the flour, baking powder, baking soda, and salt. Using the coarse side of a grater, grate the frozen butter into the flour mixture. Use your hands to rub the flour and the butter together until you have pea-size pieces. Add the buttermilk, chives, and parsley. Using a fork, bring the dough together until just combined, creating a sticky, shaggy dough. Do not overmix.

Use a scoop or a ¼-cup measuring cup to drop the dough evenly over the casserole in the baking dish. Brush the biscuits with the remaining 2 tablespoons of melted butter. Bake for 35 to 45 minutes, until the dumplings have puffed and become golden brown. Remove from the oven and let rest for 5 minutes before serving.

Yield: About 36 purses (4 to 6 servings)
V

SPECIAL TOOL:

- Pastry cutter or 3-inch square cookie cutter

BUTTERNUT SQUASH:

- 1 to 1½ pounds butternut squash
- 1 tablespoon olive oil
- 1 bulb garlic

FILLING:

- 1 cup squash purée
- 1 teaspoon salt
- Freshly ground black pepper
- 1 cup ricotta
- 1 tablespoon roasted garlic

Ingredients continue on page 109

Butternut Squash Pasta Purses

Vegetarians. We love them at the Dragonfly. (Really.) Ignore the harmless teasing. It's just that, for us, meat is less of a menu item and more of a way of life. (Lorelai loves a good breakfast cheeseburger, even if she mostly orders them to drive Luke up a wall. That, and she loves to hear him call her "hot plates.")

Yes, we're avowed carnivores. But hey—as adult professionals (adult professionals who still love anime kitten-printed socks, and?) we respect everyone's right to personal dietary choices. (What? We DO.)

Also, I am basically the Degas of fresh pasta. Ask anyone. Also, also, my produce guy is like Matisse in his world. Okay, I didn't love that pea-pea tendril switcheroo—maybe he "freestyles" a little more than I'd like. But his squash selection is A+. (Maybe stay away from the "zucchini butts," though?)

One bite of this and you might just find yourself going meatless more often! (I said "might"!)

TO MAKE THE BUTTERNUT SQUASH: Preheat the oven to 400°F.

Cut the butternut squash into four to eight pieces that are easy to handle. Use a vegetable peeler to remove the peel and a spoon to scrape out any seeds. Cut the peeled squash into ½-inch cubes. Put the olive oil and squash pieces on a rimmed baking sheet and toss the squash pieces until they are well coated in the oil, then spread out into a single layer. Cut the top off the bulb of garlic and rub the cut side on the baking sheet to oil it. Cover the baking sheet tightly with foil. Wrap the garlic bulb tightly in a smaller piece of foil. Put the baking sheet and the bulb of garlic in the oven and roast for 15 to 20 minutes or until the squash pieces are fork-tender. Roast the garlic bulb another 15 to 20 minutes or until the cloves are also fork-tender. Allow the squash and garlic to cool completely.

Reserve 1 cup of the squash cubes and purée the rest in a food processor until smooth. Squish all the roasted garlic out of the bulb into a small airtight container, work with a fork until smooth, and set aside.

Reserve ½ cup of the squash purée for making the pasta.

TO MAKE THE FILLING: In a medium mixing bowl, combine 1 cup of the squash purée, the salt, pepper to taste, the ricotta, and 1 tablespoon of the roasted garlic. Mix until smooth, cover with plastic wrap or a lid, and refrigerate until needed.

TO MAKE THE PASTA: Put 2¼ cups of the flour on a large cutting board or silicone baking mat and make a well in the middle.

In a small bowl, whisk together the egg yolks, salt, and squash purée. Add this mixture to the center of the flour well. Using a fork at first, begin incorporating flour from the edge of the well into the mixture. Once it becomes a sticky paste, switch to using your hands or a bench scraper and continue incorporating the remaining flour. If the dough is still very sticky, add up to ¼ cup of additional flour. Knead the dough, using the heels of your hands to push it away from you, until it forms a smooth ball that is no longer sticky and is elastic, 5 to 7 minutes. Wrap tightly in plastic wrap and let rest at room temperature for at least 30 minutes or up to 1 hour.

Line a baking sheet with a silicone baking mat or parchment paper. Working with a third of the dough at a time, run it through a pasta machine to create thin sheets that are almost translucent (setting 5 on many machines). Keep the portions you are not working with well wrapped so they don't dry out.

PASTA:

- 2¼ to 2½ cups double 00 flour
- 3 egg yolks
- ½ teaspoon salt
- ½ cup squash purée, from the above squash

Ingredients continue on page 110

SAUCE:

- ½ cup (8 tablespoons) salted butter
- 2 teaspoons minced fresh sage
- 1 cup squash cubes, reserved from above
- 6 to 8 small sage leaves (optional)

Using a knife, cookie cutter, or pastry wheel, cut the pasta into 3-inch squares. Place about 1 teaspoon of the filling in the center of each square. Bring the four corners together, pinching close to the filling and leaving the tops loose. Set the finished purse on the prepared baking sheet. Cover the finished purses lightly with a clean tea towel and repeat with the remaining portions of pasta. Once you've created all the purses, put the baking sheet in the refrigerator still covered with the tea towel if you're going to be cooking within 1 hour. If not, freeze the pasta purses on the baking sheet and then transfer gently to an airtight container. Cook within 1 week.

To cook the purses, bring a large pot of salted water to a boil. While the water is coming to a boil, prepare the sauce.

TO MAKE THE SAUCE: Line a plate with paper towels. In a large skillet on the stove over medium-high heat, combine the butter and minced sage. Stir the butter until it is completely melted and continue stirring as it comes to a boil. Add the reserved 1 cup of squash cubes and continue stirring for 3 minutes. Use a slotted spoon to remove the squash cubes and set them on the prepared plate. If using, add the small sage leaves. Continue stirring and cook for 1 to 2 minutes or until the leaves just begin to brown. Use the slotted spoon to transfer them to the plate with the squash cubes. Reduce the heat to medium-low and continue cooking until the solids have browned and it smells nutty (this could take up to 10 minutes, but watch carefully for the color change). Remove from the heat.

Place six to eight pasta purses in the boiling water at a time, stir gently to prevent sticking, and boil for 4 to 6 minutes or until they have all floated. Use a slotted spoon or spider to transfer the purses to the pan with the brown butter. Continue until all the purses have been cooked and added to the pan. Return the pan to the stove over medium-low heat and cook for 3 to 5 minutes, ladling the butter over the pasta purses until they are warmed through.

To serve, ladle a bit of browned butter onto each plate and top with six to eight purses. Garnish with a few squash cubes. If using, add a sage leaf to the center of one purse. Serve immediately.

Bracebridge Dinner Peacock Pie

Lorelai and I prepared this pie for the Bracebridge Dinner, where costumed servers spoke in classic Elizabethan English and we replicated an authentic period menu. (Mind you, not everyone involved was completely committed to the gig . . . Rune.) But don't worry, like with "turtleneck soup," no actual peacocks were harmed in creating this recipe.

When snow stranded our original guests in Boston (that winter weather is a very mixed blessing), we threw an out-of-control sleepover for the whole town and then some instead. The Elizabethan-ness and historical accuracy might have gotten . . . muddier as the evening wore on—but Jackson sure did look cute in his squire getup. If costumes aren't your thing? Cut straight to pie. I guarantee no one in your group of everybody will complain. This version is a medieval recipe turned into a modern-day sensation. Confit is a great make-ahead entertaining hack for this recipe or on its own.

Yield: 8 servings

SPECIAL TOOL:

- Kitchen thermometer

CONFIT:

- 4 full duck or chicken leg quarters
- 1 tablespoon kosher salt
- 6 small shallots, diced
- 6 medium cloves garlic, minced
- 4 cups rendered duck fat or olive oil
- 12 black peppercorns
- 4 bay leaves
- 1 whole sprig rosemary, cut into 3 pieces

RED WINE SAUCE:

- 1 tablespoon duck fat or olive oil from the confit
- 2 shallots or ¼ medium yellow onion, chopped
- 1 small carrot, chopped
- 1 stalk celery, chopped
- 2 cloves garlic, minced
- 2 star anise pods
- 4 whole cloves
- 1 cinnamon stick
- 1 cup red wine
- 4 sprigs thyme
- 2 bay leaves
- 2 cups beef or chicken bone broth
- Salt
- Freshly ground black pepper

Ingredients continue on page 112

TO MAKE THE CONFIT: In a large bowl or casserole dish, combine the duck, salt, shallots, and garlic. Using your hands, rub the seasoning evenly into the poultry. Cover tightly in plastic wrap and refrigerate for at least 24 hours or up to 48 hours.

Take the duck out of the refrigerator about 30 minutes to 1 hour before cooking.

Rinse the duck gently under water, pat thoroughly dry with paper towels, and place in a baking dish just large enough to hold all the pieces in a single layer. If using, gently melt the duck fat in a small pan over medium heat without letting it reach above 120°F. Pour the melted fat over the duck, making sure it is completely submerged. Distribute the peppercorns, bay leaves, and rosemary evenly, pressing them into the fat. Cover the baking dish with a lid or foil. Put in a cold oven and turn on to 275°F. Bake for 3 to 3½ hours for the duck (2 to 2½ hours for the chicken), or until the meat is completely tender. Allow to cool completely, uncovered, in the baking dish. Transfer the meat to a glass or ceramic container and strain the fat over the meat, making sure the meat is completely submerged in fat. Cover tightly and refrigerate for up to 2 weeks. (Reserve some of the confit fat to use when making the red wine sauce.)

TO MAKE THE RED WINE SAUCE: In a medium saucepan over medium-low heat, melt the confit fat. Add the shallots, carrot, celery, garlic, star anise, cloves, and cinnamon and sauté, stirring frequently, for 7 to 10 minutes, or until the vegetables are soft. Add the wine, thyme, and bay leaves, turn the

PEACOCK PIE:

- 1 recipe Quick Puff Pastry (page 26) or store-bought (see notes)
- 1 egg
- 1 teaspoon water
- 1 tablespoon olive oil
- 1 pound cremini mushrooms, sliced
- 4 sprigs thyme, plus more for garnish
- Meat from prepared 4 confit duck or chicken leg quarters
- 2 tablespoons confit fat (see notes)
- 2 large leeks, white part only, well rinsed and chopped
- 3 cloves garlic, minced
- 1 large carrot, chopped
- 1 large celery root (about 1 pound), peeled and chopped into ½-inch cubes (see notes)
- 2 teaspoons chopped fresh rosemary
- ½ teaspoon salt
- Freshly ground black pepper
- 1 cup Red Wine Sauce

TIP: Stand a chopstick in the red wine sauce and, using a rubber band, mark the amount of sauce you have before you begin reducing it. Measure occasionally until you have one-third of the original amount.

heat up to medium, and cook for 5 minutes, scraping the bottom of the pan with a spatula. Add the broth and increase the heat to high. Bring to a boil for 20 minutes, or until reduced to one-third of the original amount (see tip). Strain through a fine-mesh strainer into a bowl, pressing down gently to press out as much liquid as possible. Add salt and pepper to taste. The sauce can be made up to 5 days ahead, stored in an airtight container and refrigerated.

TO MAKE THE PEACOCK PIE: Make the puff pastry at least 2 hours before starting the filling to allow the time needed to chill, or up to 3 days in advance (see notes if using store-bought).

Place two racks in the oven, one on the bottom third and the other on the top third. Preheat the oven to 400°F, allowing an extra 15 to 20 minutes at that temperature before baking the puff pastry. Line a baking sheet with parchment paper.

Cut the puff pastry dough into eight even disks. Transfer to the prepared baking sheet.

In a small bowl, using a fork, beat the egg and water together and brush over the pastry. Prick the pastry with the fork in intervals about 1 inch apart. Bake for 12 to 15 minutes, or until golden brown, rotating the pan after 8 minutes. Put the baking sheet on a wire rack to cool completely.

Meanwhile, or up to 3 days in advance of serving, heat a large pan over medium heat. Add the oil, mushrooms, and thyme. Cover and cook for 10 minutes, or until the mushrooms release their liquid. Uncover and cook until the liquid has evaporated and the mushrooms are deeply brown, about 20 minutes. Remove from the heat, transfer to a bowl, and set aside.

While the mushrooms are cooking, remove the confit meat from the fat and leave out at room temperature. In a large heavy-bottomed pot or Dutch oven over medium-low heat, melt the confit fat. Add the leeks, garlic, carrot, celery root, and rosemary. Increase the heat to medium and sauté for 5 to 6 minutes. Add the salt and pepper to taste. Cover, lower the heat to medium-low, and cook for 15 to 20 minutes or until the vegetables are tender, stirring occasionally. Add the red wine sauce and mushrooms. Increase the heat to medium-high and cook for 5 to 7 minutes or until the sauce reduces further and coats the vegetables. Tear or cut the confit meat into bite-size pieces (about 1 inch) and add to the vegetables. Continue to sauté until heated through or store the vegetable and confit mixture in an airtight container and refrigerate for up to 3 days. (Bake the puff pastry the day you plan to serve the pie and rewarm the filling by heating it in a pan over medium-low heat. Adjust the salt and pepper as needed.)

Using a bread knife, slice each pastry in half like a bun, leaving the top and bottom whole. Place the bottom halves of the pastry on individual plates. Divide the confit filling over each pastry bottom, allowing some of the pastry to show. Place the other half of each pastry on top, slightly askew. Garnish with a sprig of thyme and serve immediately.

NOTES: If using store-bought puff pastry, cut the first sheet into six equal pieces, then cut two more pieces of equal size from the second sheet, reserving any remaining puff pastry for future use.

Any remaining confit fat can be stored in an airtight container in the refrigerator ready for your next batch of confit, roasted potatoes, or anything else benefiting from a well-seasoned oil.

Celery root is also known as celeriac. If not available, you can substitute parsnips.

Braised Lamb and Risotto

Braised lamb: delicious, and it makes an impression, though it's probably not the first thing that comes to mind for a cozy night in. But whether it's a BFF catch-up or movie date, couch meals are usually prime for those take-out menus I talked so much smack about before. (I stand by my smack, and I'll talk it again.)

But even Lorelai Gilmore—yep, the person who loves pizza so much she counts it as two of her four personal food groups, the woman who once ordered a "cheeseburger with a side of cheeseburger and a cheeseburger smoothie"—loved this dish enough to come back for seconds. Serve it for your next dinner party (there could be place cards!), then break out the leftovers for a movie marathon of your choice the next day.

Yield: 4 to 6 servings
GF*

BRAISED LAMB:

- 4 lamb shoulder chops
- 1½ teaspoons kosher salt
- ½ teaspoon freshly ground pepper
- 2 tablespoons olive oil, divided
- 1 medium yellow onion, chopped
- 3 cloves garlic, minced
- 1½ cups red wine
- ½ cup beef bone broth
- 1 tablespoon Worcestershire sauce
- 2 tablespoons tomato paste
- 2 sprigs rosemary
- 4 sprigs thyme, plus more for garnish
- 4 bay leaves

Ingredients continue on page 115

NOTE: This recipe is gluten free if using gluten-free Worcestershire sauce.

TO MAKE THE BRAISED LAMB: In a large bowl or baking dish, sprinkle the lamb with the salt and pepper. Let sit for 20 minutes.

In a large Dutch oven over medium-high heat, heat 1 tablespoon of the olive oil. Working in batches as needed, add a single layer of lamb and sear until nicely browned on all sides, 3 to 4 minutes per side, then transfer the lamb to a platter. When all the lamb has been browned and moved aside, reduce the heat to medium-low, add the remaining 1 tablespoon of olive oil, the onion, and garlic and cook, stirring often, for 5 minutes. Add the wine and cook for 5 minutes to deglaze the pan, scraping the bottom with a wooden spoon to loosen any flavorful bits. Add the broth, Worcestershire sauce, tomato paste, rosemary, thyme, and bay leaves. Increase the heat to medium-high and bring to a gentle boil, stirring to dissolve the tomato paste. Reduce the heat to low, add the lamb back in, and simmer, covered, for 2½ to 3 hours, or until fork-tender. Remove from the heat and allow to rest for 15 minutes.

Transfer the lamb to a bowl and shred it with two forks. Remove the bones and add them back to the sauce in the Dutch oven. Over medium-high heat, reduce the sauce by half by simmering it for 20 to 30 minutes. Strain the sauce over the shredded lamb. Set aside while you begin your risotto, or cool and store in an airtight container for up to 3 days. Keep warm, or reheat in a baking dish at 300°F, covered, for 25 to 30 minutes, or until heated through.

Start making the risotto 45 minutes before serving.

TO MAKE THE RISOTTO: In a medium saucepan over medium-high heat, bring the chicken broth and ½ teaspoon of salt to a boil. Reduce the heat to low and keep at a low simmer.

Meanwhile, melt 2 tablespoons of the butter in a large saucepan over medium-high heat. Add the onions and cook for 3 minutes. Add the garlic and cook for another 2 minutes. Add the rice and cook, stirring constantly, for 3 minutes. Add the wine, scraping the browned bits from the bottom of the pan. Reduce the heat to medium-low and let simmer until most of the liquid has been absorbed, about 4 minutes. Stir one ladle of the hot broth in at a time, stirring constantly between additions, and simmering until almost fully absorbed before adding another ladle of broth, about 20 minutes total, or until the rice is creamy and al dente. Add the remaining 2 tablespoons of butter, stirring vigorously until completely incorporated. Remove from the heat and stir in the crème fraîche and pecorino. Add salt and pepper to taste. Cover until ready to serve, reheating gently over low heat as needed.

To serve, distribute the risotto on the serving plates, making a dent in the middle of the risotto with the back of a large spoon. Place the lamb in the middle of the risotto and garnish with a sprig of thyme.

RISOTTO:

- 4 cups chicken bone broth (see tip)
- ½ teaspoon salt, plus more as needed
- 4 tablespoons salted or unsalted butter, divided
- 1 medium white onion, finely chopped
- 3 cloves garlic, finely minced
- 1½ cups Arborio rice
- 1 cup white wine (one you enjoy)
- ½ cup crème fraîche
- 1 cup grated pecorino or Parmesan cheese, plus more for garnish
- Freshly ground black pepper

TIP: A restaurant kitchen has room for a big pot of homemade broth simmering at all times. When possible, use bone broth to produce the richer flavor achieved by chefs.

Yield: Six 6-ounce patties
GF*

SPECIAL TOOLS:

- 3½-inch ring mold (optional)
- Meat thermometer

PATTIES:

- 1 pound skirt steak
- 1 pound boneless rib-eye steak
- 2 egg yolks
- 1 tablespoon Dijon mustard
- ½ teaspoon garlic powder
- 1 tablespoon black or mixed peppercorns, crushed (see notes)
- ¼ cup rice flour
- 1 teaspoon kosher salt
- 2 tablespoons high-heat oil, such as avocado or safflower

Ingredients continue on page 117

Steak Haché with Peppercorn Sauce

French for "chopped steak," steak haché is a little similar to a Salisbury steak or even a very, very (very!) fancy hamburger served with lots of special spices and a sauce and without a bun. It's French cuisine and even has a French name, which automatically adds at least ten fanciness points. Don't believe me? Ask Emily Gilmore, and she'll be happy to confirm. (I'm not sure why you wouldn't believe me, a classically trained and highly experienced chef, but at least we can say for sure that when it comes to Emily and etiquette, the woman knows her stuff.)*

A spicy peppercorn sauce complements the meat, and potatoes are always a perfect side.

*"Watch your clomping when you step" and "No throwing cutlery in public" are a few other Emily gems. But you can have two glasses of wine with lunch if you want. You're welcome!

TO MAKE THE PATTIES: Line a baking sheet with parchment paper.

Cut the beef into 1-inch-square pieces, place on the prepared baking sheet in a single layer, and freeze for 15 to 20 minutes or until the edges of the pieces feel frozen. Remove from the freezer and put a little at a time into the bowl of a food processor, pulsing after each addition. The mixture should look like looser, larger minced ground beef.

Transfer the mixture to a large bowl and look for any pieces that may need to be pulsed again. Add the egg yolks, mustard, and garlic powder and mix until incorporated. Using the ring mold, or your hands, shape the mixture into six equal patties. Put them back on the baking sheet.

On a large plate, combine the peppercorns, rice flour, and salt. Dredge each patty in the mixture, making sure to press the spices into the meat on both sides and covering the edges.

In a large skillet over medium-high heat, heat the oil until it coats the pan and begins to shimmer. Add the patties (you may need to do this in batches) and cook on each side until well browned, 3 to 5 minutes. The temperature will rise about 5 degrees while resting, so a temp of 130°F or 135°F will yield a medium-rare to medium finish. Remove the parchment from the baking sheet and put the cooked patties on the baking sheet. Tent the patties with foil and put in the oven or another draft-free spot while you make the sauce.

TO MAKE THE SAUCE: Add the shallots and the sage to the pan used for the patties and sauté until just beginning to soften, 3 to 5 minutes, then add the vermouth and deglaze the bottom of the pan, scraping the pan with a spoon to loosen any flavorful bits. Work in all the fond to the sauce. Continue to cook for 2 to 3 minutes, then add the beef broth and peppercorns. Bring to a simmer and continue to cook until it has reduced and begins to coat the back of a spoon, 5 to 7 minutes. Taste and add salt as needed. Whisk in the cream and cook for 1 to 2 minutes more.

To serve, make a small bed of rice, if using, ladle some sauce over it, then top with a patty, a drizzle more of sauce, and some chopped parsley.

SAUCE:

- 1 shallot, minced
- 2 teaspoons minced fresh sage
- ¼ cup sweet vermouth
- 1 cup beef broth
- 1 tablespoon black or mixed peppercorns, crushed (see notes)
- Kosher salt
- ¼ cup heavy cream

- Rice or pasta, for serving (optional)
- 2 tablespoons chopped parsley, for garnish

NOTES: The peppercorns can be a mix of black, pink, white, or green, but black should make up the bulk of the mixture. Crush the peppercorns with a mortar and pestle. The consistency should be much coarser than ground pepper but without whole peppercorns.

This sauce also works well with your favorite steak, or ask the butcher to make the minced mixture for you.

This recipe is gluten free if served with rice or gluten-free pasta.

Yield: 8 to 10 servings
GF*

SPECIAL TOOL:

- Meat thermometer

- 3 to 4 pounds boneless prime rib roast or eye round roast
- 2½ teaspoons salt, divided
- 1 teaspoon whole peppercorns, crushed (see notes)
- 1 tablespoon chopped fresh rosemary (about 2 sprigs)
- 2 tablespoons finely minced garlic (about 8 medium cloves)
- 1 cup beef bone broth
- ½ cup cognac or brandy
- 2 tablespoons tomato paste
- 2 tablespoons unsalted butter, softened
- 2 tablespoons extra-virgin olive oil
- 1 large (or 2 small) shallot, minced
- 8 ounces mushrooms, sliced
- ½ cup heavy cream
- 3 tablespoons Dijon mustard
- 1 tablespoon Worcestershire sauce
- Freshly ground black pepper
- 1 tablespoon finely chopped fresh flat-leaf parsley

Baron of Beef with Sauce Diane

Perfect for a holiday feast or any old time you want to feed (and impress!) a crowd, this hunk of meat is truly fit for royalty. Another runaway from our first (and still only) Bracebridge Dinner, the original version of this recipe called for "thirty pounds of aged beef" (but you can adjust for scale).

One out of one Richard Gilmores agrees that a grown man cannot subsist on fish alone (we can get into the apple/tree thing re: Luke's burgers later). If this giant portion of beef tenderloin feels like a lot for a random Friday night dinner, freeze leftovers in single servings for smart meal prep (and another chance to ditch the take-out menus). And as a Christmas dinner main? Now we're firmly in Emily Gilmore—and apple tart—territory.

Fun fact: We cheated on this one because technically roux didn't exist in ye olden tymes . . . Shhh!

Pat the roast dry with paper towels.

In a small bowl, combine 2 teaspoons of the salt, the peppercorns, rosemary, and garlic. Spread the garlic mixture all over the top and sides of the roast, with the fat side being the top. Wrap the roast in plastic wrap, place in a baking dish to catch leaks, and refrigerate for at least 2 hours but preferably overnight.

Preheat the oven to 500°F. Prepare a roasting pan with a wire rack inside.

Remove the plastic wrap from the roast. Place the roast, fat-side up, on the wire rack. Let sit out on the counter for 30 minutes while the oven is preheating. Place the roast into the hot oven and reduce the temperature immediately to 450°F. Roast for 15 minutes, reduce the temperature to 325°F, and continue to roast for 15 to 20 minutes per pound. Use a meat thermometer, inserting it into the thickest part of the roast, to check that the internal temperature is 125°F to 130°F for rare, or 130°F to 140°F for medium, roasting for longer as needed.

While the meat is roasting, in a medium saucepan over low heat, simmer the broth until reduced by half, 20 to 30 minutes. Set aside.

Once the desired internal temperature of the roast has been reached, remove the roast from the oven. Transfer it to a serving platter or cutting board, tent with foil, and let rest for 15 to 20 minutes before slicing.

While the roast is resting, remove the wire rack from the roasting pan. While the roasting pan is still hot, add the cognac and the reduced beef broth. Using a spatula, scrape the bottom of the roasting pan. Return the broth mixture to the medium saucepan. Bring to a boil over medium-high heat. Reduce the temperature to medium-low and simmer for 7 to 10 minutes, or until it begins to thicken. Whisk in the tomato paste and simmer for 3 minutes.

Meanwhile, in a large skillet over medium-low heat, melt the butter with the olive oil. Add the shallots and cook, stirring, for 30 seconds. Add the mushrooms and cook for 15 minutes. Add the remaining ½ teaspoon of salt and sauté for another 2 minutes. Stir in the broth mixture and cream and simmer, stirring, for 2 minutes. Stir in the mustard, Worcestershire sauce, pepper to taste, and any of the juice from the roast accumulating on the platter or cutting board and simmer for another 5 to 10 minutes, or until it is thick enough to coat a spoon. Set aside until ready to serve, reheating over medium-low heat as needed. Just before serving, stir in the parsley. Serve with the sliced roast.

NOTES: To crush whole peppercorns, use a mortar and pestle or put them on a large cutting board and press the bottom of a heavy pan into them until they break up into coarse pieces.

This recipe is gluten free if using gluten-free Worcestershire sauce.

Chapter Six: Drinks, Cocktails & Mixes

Wassail

Wassail-ing away!

It's a thing you do! It's a thing you drink! It's a million different holiday traditions rolled into one cozy, cinnamon-spicy, pour-yourself-a-mug-and-take-a-leisurely-caroling-with-friends-stroll-past-the-gazebo-y holiday beverage.

The word wassail is a little confusing—kinda like "Smurf," it can be any part of the sentence. But it's got a long history—Professor Interwebs says you can even draw a line from wassail straight to eggnog, by some accounts. Early settlers supposedly drank a version of it while wandering in the woods, shouting to ward off evil spirits. (Should we have tried that for Lorelai's termites?)

Don't tell Taylor, though. It feels like something he'd try to reenact, and we're already so full up on quirky traditions and stuff, you know? I served this version at our Bracebridge Dinner alongside Plum Pudding with Hard Sauce (page 140), and it was a hit.

Yield: 6 to 8 servings
V, V+, GF*

- 8 cups apple cider or apple juice, preferably unfiltered
- 1 orange, thinly sliced
- 2 lemons, thinly sliced
- 4 cinnamon sticks
- 12 whole cloves
- 4 star anise pods
- 2-inch piece ginger, peeled and roughly chopped
- 2 tablespoons maple syrup
- ½ cup bourbon (optional)

In a large pot over medium-low heat, combine the cider, orange slices, lemon slices, cinnamon sticks, cloves, star anise, ginger pieces, and maple syrup. Bring to a simmer, reduce the heat to low, and simmer for 45 minutes more. Serve hot or warm, adding the bourbon as you serve or offering it on the side, if using.

NOTE: This recipe is gluten free if using gluten-free bourbon.

TIP: Spike it for the 21+ set if you're feeling extra wassail.

"Enscotched" Cocktail

Yield: 2 servings
V, V+, GF*

- 1 orange
- 4 ounces Scotch
- 2 tablespoons liquid from Brandied Cherries (page 16)
- Ice
- 2 Brandied Cherries (page 16)

NOTE: This recipe is gluten free if using gluten-free Scotch.

Necessity is the mother of invention . . . and wow, are you guys in luck. I invented this drink the year Jackson decided we'd deep-fry a turkey in the backyard for Thanksgiving . . . and then tried to deep-fry everything else he could get his hands on, too. (Even the napkins.)

Boy, did I ever necessity some kind of . . . consoling-ish thing to . . . console me, then! (OH! "Consolation prize" is the phrase I was looking for!) I plowed right through the five stages of grief that Thanksgiving—denial, anger . . . one or two I forget now—or maybe never knew in the first place—that were served on the rocks, I think? . . . With a salted rim? Then I settled into a nice place of comfortable "enscotchment"—tucked away in blissful, willful oblivion.

The brandied cherry liquid smooths out the Scotch, easing you into enscotched bliss . . . No deep-frying necessary.

Cut off one end of the orange. Cut two thin slices to use as garnish and juice the rest.

In a cocktail shaker or jar, combine the orange juice, Scotch, and brandied cherry liquid. Fill two glasses with ice. Pour the Scotch mixture over the ice.

Cut a slit, starting from the middle of each orange slice, down through the rind. Twist the orange slice, skewering a cherry into each fold of the orange. Place on top of each glass and serve immediately.

Four Years without a Cocktail Mockaritas

Yield: 2 servings
V, V+, GF

- 5 limes, scrubbed clean
- 2 tablespoons kosher or pink Himalayan salt
- 1 orange, scrubbed clean
- 2 cups water
- 2 tablespoons agave nectar or simple syrup, plus more as needed
- Ice

If Emily Gilmore can handle the switch to mocktails in the name of her husband's health, I can teetotal with a "mockarita" while I'm pregnant. Right?

Of course, Lorelai didn't count on her mother insisting everyone go booze-free alongside Richard. And I hadn't really thought about what Jackson's plan for "four in four" would mean for me, my body, or my dietary habits. (Never did love the whole math thing; it makes my head hurt.)

Four kids in four years is also basically four straight years on the wagon . . . and we may love our old-timey charm here in Stars Hollow, but there's a reason the combustion engine was invented, y'know? Not to mention what pregnancy does to my palate, which isn't always ideal for a chef . . .

Anyway. What I'm saying is you can keep your covered wagon, buster. Especially for four straight years. But . . . Sometimes the occasion calls for something refreshing and nonalcoholic. Your reasons are your own, so have at it. Serve on the rocks, with lots of salt on the rim. And a word of friendly advice? If you have opinions about your best friend's husband's family planning . . . keep them to yourself. And if four whole years without a cocktail is just too much for you? Feel free to add tequila or Pineapple-Infused Vodka (page 136) and make this mockarita an adults-only beverage.

Zest one of the limes. In a shallow bowl, wider than your glasses, mix the zest with the salt. Set aside to use on the rims.

Cut the ends off the zested lime, three of the other limes, and the orange. Cut each of these fruits into eight wheels and remove any visible seeds. Put the cut limes, orange, water, and agave in a blender. Pulse four or five times. It should be very chunky. Pour through a fine-mesh strainer into a large measuring cup, pressing down gently on the pulp to extract as much juice as possible. Taste the liquid in the measuring cup, adding more agave as needed.

Cut the remaining lime into slices and cut a slit into each one from the middle of the slice down. Wet the rims of the glasses with one of the slices or water and press the glass upside down into the lime salt. Add ice to each glass and pour the mockarita over the ice. Garnish each glass with a lime slice and serve immediately.

Stars Hollow Party Punch

. . . Because, really, you don't want to have to drink something that tastes like a magical pink unicorn/pony sparkle toy—even if Luke Danes will forever be the original grumpy old man, no matter what age he actually is. (Do you think he hung a tiny NO CELL PHONES sign in utero?)

Make a batch of this punch for your next potluck and you'll know the beverage options will be up to par. Then you can focus on all the little details, like making sure the candles are all spaced exactly six inches apart. (Kidding.)

Now, some of your more "memorable" party punches are born of pure whimsy slash whatever you've got in the fridge and bar cart. (Ask Rory about her experiences on spring break with Paris.) It gets the job done, but it doesn't always end well. This recipe is grown-up punch: bright and fruity. Whip up a batch before your next bash. Boas optional (BYO)—but always strongly encouraged.

Yield: 12 servings
V, V+, GF

- 4 cups cranberry-raspberry or plain cranberry juice
- 2 cups pineapple juice
- ⅔ cup freshly squeezed lemon juice (about 4 lemons)
- ¼ cup Ginger Syrup (page 129) (see notes)
- 1 or 2 oranges, thinly sliced
- 1 lemon, thinly sliced (optional)
- 1 cup raspberries or sliced strawberries
- 1½ cups Pineapple-Infused Vodka (page 136) (optional)
- 2 or 3 cups ice
- 4 cups sparkling apple cider or seltzer (see notes)

In a large pitcher, combine the cranberry-raspberry juice, pineapple juice, lemon juice, and ginger syrup. Add the sliced oranges and lemons, raspberries, and vodka (if using) and stir well.

If making ahead, refrigerate for 2 to 24 hours, covered with a lid or plastic wrap. Just before serving, add the ice and top with the sparkling cider.

NOTES: You can replace the ginger syrup and seltzer with 4 cups of ginger ale.

If you don't have a gallon-size pitcher, make the base and add ice and the sparkling cider or seltzer in batches or individual glasses.

This recipe is gluten free if using gluten-free vodka in the Pineapple-Infused Vodka.

Remember costumes for Patty by Fri.
—Lorelai

Ginger Fizz

Feeling festive? Sure, you could go the traditional route for your toasting purposes—champagne or anything bubbly. No one would question it, it's the obvious choice . . . which isn't a bad thing.

But—not bad? Not bad? Come on—I know you can do better than that. And it's always extra fun to customize a cocktail for a special occasion, like Emily did for Rory's 21st birthday. (Did it make up for the fact that Lorelai and Rory weren't in Vegas, playing 21 at the exact very moment Rory turned 21, like they'd been planning forever? Nope. But that was a pretty tall order. Like cute-first-love-and-cookies-Dean tall. Reconciliation-between-mother-and-daughter-was-never-gonna-happen-in-time-for-that tall.)

Dean was very tall. And so cute. I shouldn't use past tense—he's probably still the same height. What a great first boyfriend that guy was for Rory. What was I talking about? Right, festive things!

Here's an easy, spicy twist on a bottle of boring-old-regular bubbly. This take uses ginger simple syrup and delightfully refreshing prosecco. Prost!

Yield: 5 or 6 servings; about 1¼ cups ginger syrup

V, V+, GF

GINGER SYRUP:

- 7-inch piece fresh ginger (about 4 ounces), peeled and coarsely chopped
- 1 cup water
- 1 cup granulated sugar

DRINK:

- 3 to 6 ounces Ginger Syrup
- 1 bottle prosecco or champagne, chilled

TO MAKE THE GINGER SYRUP: In a medium saucepan over medium-high heat, combine the ginger, water, and sugar and stir until the sugar is dissolved, about 5 minutes. Reduce the heat to medium-low and simmer for 8 to 10 minutes, stirring occasionally. Cover and set aside in a cool place for 12 to 24 hours. Strain the liquid into a 12-ounce jar through a fine-mesh strainer, removing the ginger and pressing down gently to remove as much liquid as possible. Store refrigerated in a bottle or jar for up to 3 weeks.

TO MAKE THE DRINK: Place 1 tablespoon of the ginger syrup at the bottom of each champagne flute. Pour the prosecco over the syrup. Offer extra on the side. Serve immediately.

Yield: 6 servings; 2 cups bacon-infused vodka
GF*

BACON-INFUSED VODKA:

- 6 ounces bacon
- 2 cups vodka

Ingredients continue on page 131

Jazz hands should always be a given.
—Miss Patty

Bacon-Infused Vodka Bloody Mary

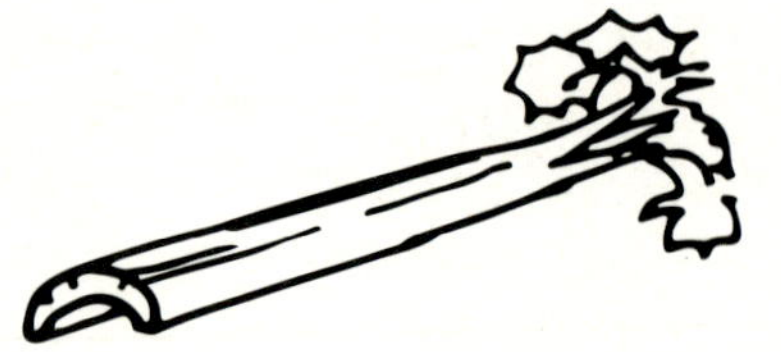

There's a reason a Bloody Mary is a classic brunch cocktail. Whether you're in the mood for a little supercool-party-people-Sunday-Funday-day-drink buzz, or you woke up buck naked on the floor of your college dorm hallway and now you're in desperate need of a little hair of the dog that bit you—a Bloody Mary is 100 percent the brunch drink to reach for every time. The spicy bite of tomato and herbs will perk you right up. Something for everyone!

So I asked everyone—everyone we know, like, I mean, everyone everyone—if there's anything they'd do to crank a Bloody Mary up to eleven. Just a casual little straw poll. And it turns out there is one thing all citizens of Stars Hollow agree on (even Taylor!). The one thing that makes everything better, always? Bacon.

Bacon, bacon, bacon! Make up a song! You can add jazz hands! Suddenly, life's fun; suddenly, there's a reason to get up in the morning! It's called bacon! And it belongs in your drink!

At least wipe the bacon grease off them before you start waving your fingers in other people's faces.
—Michel

TO MAKE THE BACON-INFUSED VODKA: Preheat the oven to 375°F. Line a baking sheet with foil.

Put the bacon slices on the prepared baking sheet. Bake for 15 to 20 minutes, or until golden brown. Remove the bacon from the oven and allow it to cool for 15 minutes. Stuff the bacon into a 2½- to 3-cup jar. Pour the bacon fat over the bacon. Add the vodka and seal tightly with a lid. Let the vodka sit for 7 to 10 days, shaking occasionally.

When ready to strain, remove the layer of bacon fat from the top and discard. Using a rubber band, attach a coffee filter to the top of a 2- to 2½-cup mason jar, fitting it so the bulk of the filter is inside the jar. Place a fine-mesh strainer over the top of the filter and strain the vodka through both the strainer and the coffee filter, refilling as needed. Clean out the strainer as needed. (This can take 24 hours or more because the bacon fat starts to coat the filter, so plan ahead or replace the paper filter once or twice as needed.) Place a lid over the jar as it is straining and walk away for a few hours, adding more of the bacon vodka as it filters through. Store, refrigerated, for up to 3 months.

TO MAKE THE BLOODY MARY: In a large pitcher, combine the tomato juice, lemon juice, pickle juice, and Worcestershire sauce. Stir well. Add the horseradish to taste, hot sauce to taste, celery salt, and pepper, adjusting to taste. Add the vodka and stir well. This can be made up to 2 days ahead and stored in an airtight container in the refrigerator. Shake or stir before continuing.

If including a salt rim, put the kosher salt on a small plate. Wet the rims of each glass and place the glass upside down on the salt, twisting to get it on evenly. Add ice to the glasses and pour in the Bloody Mary. Garnish with a celery stalk and bacon, if using, and serve immediately.

BLOODY MARY:

- 3 cups tomato juice
- Juice from 2 lemons (about ⅔ cup)
- ½ cup pickle juice
- 2 tablespoons Worcestershire sauce (optional)
- 2 to 3 tablespoons horseradish
- ½ to 1 teaspoon hot sauce
- 1 teaspoon celery salt
- ¼ teaspoon freshly ground black pepper
- 12 ounces Bacon-Infused Vodka
- 2 tablespoons kosher salt, for the rim (optional)
- Ice
- 6 stalks celery, for garnish (optional)
- 6 slices bacon, for garnish (optional)

NOTE: This recipe can be made gluten free by choosing gluten-free Worcestershire sauce and vodka.

Yield: 4 servings; 2 cups coffee-infused vodka; 1 cup coffee syrup
V, GF*

COFFEE-INFUSED VODKA:

- ½ cup coffee grounds (regular or decaf)
- 2 cups vodka

COFFEE SYRUP:

- 1 cup granulated sugar
- 1 cup espresso, extra-strong brewed coffee, or cold-brew concentrate

MARTINI:

- ½ cup heavy cream
- 2 tablespoons powdered sugar
- ½ teaspoon espresso powder
- ½ teaspoon vanilla extract
- 8 ounces Coffee-Infused Vodka
- 1 cup Coffee Syrup
- 1 cup ice
- 12 chocolate-covered coffee beans, whole or roughly chopped, for garnish (optional)

Call re: rental sleighs? —Lorelai

NOTE: This recipe is gluten free as long as you choose a gluten-free vodka.

"Coffee! Coffee! Coffee!" Martini

Five cups a day is my business partner and best friend's standard intake. That's normal, right? We're talking baseline. I've given up trying to intervene and have moved onto enabling. Look, everyone has their vices.

So maybe the barista at Weston didn't recognize Lorelai's little "bit" about her caffeine habit, but she's probably the only person in Stars Hollow who wouldn't.

This cocktail is perfect for a girls' night. For those of us who—like Lorelai—like our coffee "only with our oxygen," it's the perfect blend of a full-bodied dark roast and a crisp vodka martini. Add whipped topping for flair—not that you and your BFF don't have flair enough on your own. Absolutely not. You two are stuffed to the brim with flair! You've got flair to spare! You're downright devil-may-care with flair!

Now that I think about it, I had a lot of the coffee bean garnish testing out this recipe.

TO MAKE THE COFFEE-INFUSED VODKA: Pour the coffee and vodka into a large 2½- to 3-cup jar. Seal with a lid and shake. Allow to sit for 7 to 10 days at room temperature, shaking the jar every day or two. Strain into a large measuring cup or medium bowl using a coffee filter or fine-mesh strainer. Transfer to a jar or bottle and store in the refrigerator for up to 6 months.

TO MAKE THE COFFEE SYRUP: In a small saucepan over medium-high heat, combine the granulated sugar and coffee. Bring to a boil, stirring until the sugar has completely dissolved, about 5 minutes. Lower the heat to medium-low and simmer for 3 minutes. Set aside to cool for 10 minutes before transferring the syrup to a jar or bottle. Once it has cooled completely, cover and refrigerate for at least 2 hours, or up to 1 week.

TO MAKE THE MARTINI: Put a medium mixing bowl and beaters or whisk attachment for a hand mixer in the freezer for 10 minutes. Remove the bowl from the freezer. In the chilled bowl, combine the cream, powdered sugar, espresso powder, and vanilla. Beat until the cream has thickened substantially but is still pourable. Use immediately with your coffee martini or refrigerate for up to 4 hours.

In a cocktail shaker or jar, shake the vodka and coffee syrup to combine. Add the ice and shake vigorously until well chilled. Strain the liquid into four martini glasses and top with the whipped cream. Garnish with the chocolate-covered coffee beans, if using. Serve immediately.

Garnish with
chocolate-covered
coffee beans!

Chocolate Chocolate Chip Milkshake

Yield: 2 servings
V, GF*

- 4 tablespoons chocolate syrup, divided, plus more for garnish
- 1 to 1½ cups whole milk, depending on desired thickness (see notes)
- 1 pint chocolate chocolate chip ice cream
- ¾ cup heavy cream

Technically, it was a termite infestation that brought Lorelai and Rory to my yard—er, my house—on a random weekday midnight. Who—who, I ask you?—could sleep knowing those little creepers were chittering through the walls, crawling and skittering all over, with their fangy teeth and their pointy tentacles . . . ? (We might not know what termites look like.)

But who cares what the reason was? If you crash at Auntie Sookie's house, we're going to have the ultimate slumber party! Face masks, tarot readings, Twister . . . Let's go! It only takes about twenty to thirtyish rings for the phone to rouse me.

Lorelai appreciated the hospitality but pointed out that it was a little late for all of that hoopla. I suggested we cut straight to the milkshakes instead. Chocolate chips, chocolate syrup, chocolate ice cream, chocolate whipped cream . . . you get it. Just your basic chocolate-covered hoopla package.

Put 1 tablespoon of the chocolate syrup into the bottom of each of two tall glasses. Place the glasses in the freezer until needed.

In a blender, briefly pulse the remaining 2 tablespoons of chocolate syrup and 1 cup of the milk. Add the ice cream and blend until fully incorporated. Add the remaining milk, 1 tablespoon at a time, to achieve your desired consistency.

Place the heavy cream into a whipped cream canister or small mixing bowl and use a hand mixer to beat until still peaks form.

Remove the glasses from the freezer. Split the milkshake between the two glasses, leaving a 1-inch gap at the top of each. Top each glass with a tower of whipped cream and drizzle with additional chocolate syrup to garnish. Serve immediately with a long spoon, straw, or both.

NOTES: One cup of milk will make a thick, spoon-worthy milkshake. Reserve the additional ½ cup of milk to thin as desired.

*This recipe is gluten free as long as you choose gluten-free ice cream and syrup.

Homemade Eggnog

Yield: 6 to 8 servings
V, GF

I know, I know—any drink involving the word <u>egg</u> can be a little divisive (see also: egg <u>cream</u>, the old-school soda fountain drink, which Lorelai first had doubts about, too—until she found out there was chocolate involved). But if you're wary, it's just because you haven't tried mine from scratch. (Any excuse to break out the hand whisk!)

Even Paris Geller calls eggnog "disgusting—in a really great way." And we all know she can be a <u>scooch</u> grinch-y. (With an extra dusting of nutmeg, a glass of this to drink by her very own Hanukkah bush will have her donning holly-colored glasses.)

This is a drink that sings "fa-la-la-la-la" for sure. But you can enjoy yours beside a cozy nondenominational fire and/or the seasonal shrub of your choice. I promise—there's <u>nog-ging</u> else like it on a postcard-perfect winter night!

SPECIAL TOOL:

- Candy thermometer

- 6 eggs, separated
- ¾ cup granulated sugar, divided
- 4 cups whole milk
- 2 teaspoons vanilla paste

NOTE: This pairs very well with bourbon and whiskey. If you plan on serving plain or with a sweeter liqueur such as brandy, you may want to reduce the sugar.

In a heavy-bottomed saucepan, whisk together the egg yolks and ½ cup of the sugar until thick and pale, 2 to 3 minutes. Put the saucepan over medium-low heat, whisk in the milk, and fit the saucepan with the candy thermometer. Stir almost constantly until the temperature reaches 170°F.

While the milk mixture is cooking, put the egg whites in the bowl of a stand mixer or a large mixing bowl if using a hand mixer and mix on high speed until the eggs are frothy. Slowly add the remaining ¼ cup of sugar with the mixer still running and continue to mix until stiff peaks form.

Once the milk mixture reaches 170°F, remove it from the heat and whisk in the egg whites in three batches. Return the pan to the stove over low heat and continue whisking until the entire mixture has been at least 160°F but no hotter than 170°F for 5 minutes.

Remove from the heat again, whisk in the vanilla, and pour into a heatproof container. Refrigerate for at least 6 hours or overnight.

Weather report? Smelling snowy.
—Lorelai

Yield: 2 servings;
1 to 1½ cups pineapple-infused vodka
V, V+, GF*

PINEAPPLE-INFUSED VODKA:

- 2 cups pineapple chunks
- 1 to 1½ cups vodka

FOR THE DRINK:

- 2 limes
- 4 ounces Pineapple-Infused Vodka
- 2 to 4 tablespoons Ginger Syrup (page 129)
- Ice
- 4 Brandied Cherries (page 16) (optional)

NOTE: This recipe can be made gluten free by choosing a gluten-free vodka.

SMAD?
–LUKE

It's a portmanteau. Two words combined.
—Rory

Smad = sad + mad. Like motel, or spork. Any day now all the cool kids'll be saying it. Just you wait.
—Lorelai

Ennui / Off-oui, "Oh, Hey, I'm Cured!" Cocktail

How does that saying go? Into every life a little smadness may fall.

Now, I'm a pretty chipper person most of the time. I like to keep it peppy in my kitchen, with the singing, and the laughter, and the minimal number of mishaps (it was just that one time my stitches opened while I was saving the peach sauce, Lorelai). My kitchen is a pretty perky place. (Pretty perky peppy place. Try saying that ten times fast. Give it a little beat. You could even dance to it . . . ?)

But every now and then, some of us can experience a little . . . ennui. (Three guesses which Dragonfly employee is most likely to feel it.) For those days when you're feeling very serious—maybe even Jean-Paul-Sartre serious?—if you're looking to lighten things up, this cocktail is my go-to cure for what ails you. With a punch of pineapple, a kick of ginger simple syrup, and garnished with a lime slice, one sip will wash that ennui away.

So what does that leave you with? The opposite of ennui: off-oui! Ha! That one gets me every time.

TO MAKE THE PINEAPPLE-INFUSED VODKA: Put the pineapple in a 2- to 3-cup jar. Pour the vodka over the pineapple to cover completely. Cover tightly with a lid and let sit at room temperature for 1 to 2 weeks, or until the vodka flavor reaches your preferred taste. Strain through a fine-mesh strainer into a jar and discard the pineapple. Store refrigerated for up to 2 weeks.

TO MAKE THE DRINK: Cut two slices from one of the limes and juice the rest. In a cocktail shaker, combine the vodka, lime juice, and 2 tablespoons of the ginger syrup. Shake, taste, and add more ginger syrup as desired. Pour over two glasses filled with ice and garnish with the cherries (if using) and reserved lime slices. Serve immediately.

I do so enjoy lazy wordplay made at my own expense. Thank you; this will do wonders for my existential despair.
—Michel

Chapter Seven: Desserts

Yield: 6 servings
V

SPECIAL TOOLS:

- Six 6-ounce ramekins
- Butter molds (optional)

PLUM PUDDING:

- ½ cup diced dried fig
- ½ cup dried cherries
- ½ cup diced prunes
- ½ cup diced candied ginger
- 1 cup boiling water
- 1½ cups all-purpose flour
- 1 teaspoon baking powder
- 2 teaspoons ground cinnamon
- ½ teaspoon ground allspice
- ¼ teaspoon ground cloves
- ½ teaspoon salt
- ½ cup (8 tablespoons) unsalted butter, softened, plus more for greasing
- 1 cup packed dark brown sugar
- 3 eggs

HARD SAUCE:

- ½ cup (8 tablespoons) salted butter
- 1¼ cups powdered sugar
- 2 tablespoons dark rum

Plum Pudding with Hard Sauce

A plum delicious finale to any meal! Yet another Bracebridge creation—the historical reenactment dinner that keeps on giving! It's not "pudding," like Emily Gilmore served out of absolute nowhere to Lorelai and Rory one random Friday night just to keep everyone on their toes. (Was she trying to show the girls she was making an effort to understand them? Was it some newfangled but insidious type of psychological warfare? We'll never know for sure.)

No, this is plum pudding the way in England pudding refers to "dessert." Think rice or bread. I like to serve it in mini ramekins, individually steamed, so everyone gets their own pretty little pot. A pretty little personal pot of plum pudding. What could be more perfectly picturesque for your penultimate* course?

*Yes, I know your dessert could be your ultimate course, not penultimate. Shush. Do I come to your job and critique your wordplay?

TO MAKE THE PUDDING: In a heatproof bowl, combine the fig, cherries, prunes, and ginger and cover with the boiling water. Let stand for 15 minutes.

In a small mixing bowl, mix together the flour, baking powder, cinnamon, allspice, cloves, and salt. Set aside.

Drain the fruit over a bowl, reserving both the fruit and the liquid. Toss the fruit in a mixing bowl with ¼ cup of the flour mixture. Set aside.

Preheat the oven to 375°F, grease the ramekins with butter, and set them in a 9-by-13-inch casserole dish.

In the bowl of a stand mixer fitted with a paddle attachment or a large mixing bowl if using a hand mixer, combine the butter and the brown sugar on high speed until light and fluffy, about 2 minutes. Add the eggs one at a time, mixing on medium speed after each addition.

Add half of the remaining flour mixture and mix on low speed, then scrape down the sides of the bowl. Add the reserved fruit liquid and mix again, still on low speed, ending with the remaining flour. Mix again on low speed until all the flour is incorporated. Remove the bowl from the stand mixer, if using, scrape down the sides, and fold in the fruit.

NOTE: The puddings can be made ahead, cooled, and then refrigerated for up to 1 week or frozen for up to 1 month. Wrap in plastic wrap or store between layers of parchment paper in an airtight container. To reheat, place them back in their molds and follow the steaming instructions below. Steam for 30 to 40 minutes or until a knife inserted in the center feels hot to the touch.

Divide the batter among the ramekins, filling each about three-quarters full.

Fill the baking dish with hot water until the water level is halfway up the ramekins, and cover the whole dish with foil. Carefully place in the oven and bake for 45 to 50 minutes or until set. Remove from the oven and transfer the ramekins to a wire rack. Serve warm in the ramekins or, to unmold, run a knife around the edge of the pudding, cover with a plate, and invert to unmold.

TO MAKE THE HARD SAUCE: While the puddings are in the oven, in a medium mixing bowl or the bowl of a stand mixer, combine the butter, powdered sugar, and rum and beat on medium speed until smooth. Either spread into butter molds or wrap in plastic wrap, forming it into a log. Refrigerate until firm, about 30 minutes. Serve the warm puddings with either a few pieces of molded hard sauce or a slice of it from the log.

Yield: 6 servings
GF

SPECIAL TOOLS:

- Six 10-ounce glass dessert cups or ramekins

CANDIED KUMQUATS:

- 12 ounces kumquats
- ¼ cup water
- ½ cup granulated sugar
- ½ teaspoon unflavored gelatin
- 12 fresh raspberries, for garnish

Ingredients continue on page 143

Raspberry Mousse with Candied Kumquats and Kumquat Gelée

Jackson Belleville. Let me tell you about Jackson Belleville. The man's quirky. And a little presumptuous. We all know I don't love when someone brings me pea shoot tendrils instead of Brussels sprouts or blueberries instead of strawberries, just because he decided—all on his own—he didn't like the looks of whatever I actually asked for that week. (I can't make a strawberry shortcake with blueberries, no matter how hard I try, and I can't make that sound like good news to Lorelai, either!)

(Of course, I can make a blueberry shortcake—and I did! Because I'm just that amazing! Still, though. I ordered strawberries.)

Anyway, Jackson. Presumptuous, yes. But when it comes to produce, the man is a god. A god, I say! Laugh all you want—he built a hothouse that frees us from the limits of the natural farming seasons, and he's a whiz with hybrids. Now, behold: the rasquat! And now, you can be-taste: the dessert worthy of his adventures in food science—a light, airy mousse sure to shut those naysayers right up. Long live the rasquat!

TO MAKE THE CANDIED KUMQUATS: Line a baking sheet with parchment paper.

Slice 14 of the kumquats into thin rounds, carefully removing the seeds from the rounds. Cut the remaining kumquats in half and juice them. In a medium saucepan over low heat, combine the sliced kumquats, kumquat juice, water, and sugar. Stir until the sugar has completely dissolved, 5 to 7 minutes, and then increase the heat to medium and bring to a simmer. Continue to simmer for 15 minutes.

Remove from the heat and strain over a glass measuring cup. Reserve the liquid and set aside. Spread the kumquat slices out in a single layer onto the prepared baking sheet. Set aside to dry.

Sprinkle the gelatin over the reserved kumquat syrup and allow to bloom for 5 minutes. Once the gelatin has bloomed, return the kumquat syrup to the saucepan and heat gently over medium-low until all the gelatin has dissolved. Set aside to cool.

Gently wash and dry the raspberries and set them in a mini muffin cup or silicone mold to hold them upright. Use a small spoon to fill the center of each raspberry with the kumquat gelée and cap off with a piece of candied kumquat. Refrigerate until ready to serve.

TO MAKE THE RASPBERRY MOUSSE: In a medium saucepan over low heat, mash together the raspberries and sugar. Stir until the sugar is completely dissolved, 7 to 10 minutes, then increase the heat to medium and bring to a low boil. Continue to boil, stirring frequently, for about 5 minutes or until thickened.

Remove from the heat and strain through a chinois or fine-mesh strainer into a bowl to remove all the seeds. Set aside to cool completely.

In the bowl of a stand mixer fitted with a whisk attachment or a large mixing bowl if using a hand mixer, whip the mascarpone cheese on high speed until light and fluffy, about 2 minutes. Add the raspberry syrup and mix again on high speed until fully incorporated and fluffy, 1 to 2 minutes, scraping down the sides of the bowl as needed.

In a separate large mixing bowl, use a hand mixer to whip the cream on high speed until stiff peaks form. In three batches, gently fold the raspberry mixture, and orange blossom water, if using, into the whipped cream mixture until no streaks remain. Divide the mixture among the dessert cups, leaving 1 inch of space at the top. Arrange slices of candied kumquat and cover with a very thin layer of the gelée (about 2 tablespoons for each cup). Refrigerate for at least 2 hours before serving.

RASPBERRY MOUSSE:

- 10 ounces frozen raspberries (see note)
- 1 cup granulated sugar
- 8 ounces mascarpone cheese
- 1½ cups heavy cream
- ½ teaspoon orange blossom water (optional)

NOTE: If using fresh raspberries, allow the raspberries to sit in a medium-size bowl with the sugar and macerate for 30 minutes before adding to the pot.

Sour Cream Peach Pie

Yield: About 8 servings
V, GF*

This is one of my signature pies, ever since those early days of rolling Jackson's peaches across the floor of the Independence Inn, checking for wateriness. (Oh, he loved it. All that kvetching and moaning was just for show. Trust me, I know my Jackson. He would've done the same thing if our roles were reversed. Nobody likes a watery peach.)

Jackson volunteered my baking skills for Rory's farewell party—he knows me just as well as I know him. Even if Taylor's secret party planning meeting wasn't an "official" meeting according to Robert's Rules, the pie had no "opposed" votes. (And it's not like I'm waiting on a quorum's consensus to bake Rory a pie!)

The sour cream in the pie adds an extra little zing here, and who doesn't love some zing? (Serving this pie with vanilla ice cream on the side wouldn't be the worst idea, either. Just saying. Zing zap kablammo!)

PEACH FILLING:

- 4 cups sliced peaches (4 to 6 fresh peaches or 20 ounces frozen peaches)
- ¼ cup granulated sugar
- 1 tablespoon tapioca flour
- ½ teaspoon ground cinnamon
- ¼ cup lemon juice

CRUST:

- 2 cups cookie crumbs (about 12 ounces cookies)
- 1 tablespoon packed light brown sugar
- 5 tablespoons unsalted butter, melted

SOUR CREAM MIXTURE:

- ¾ cup granulated sugar
- 3 egg yolks
- ½ cup sour cream
- 1 tablespoon tapioca flour
- 1 teaspoon vanilla paste

NOTE: This can be made gluten free by using gluten-free cookies for the crust.

Preheat the oven to 350°F.

TO MAKE THE PEACH FILLING: In a large saucepot over medium-high heat, combine the peaches, granulated sugar, tapioca flour, cinnamon, and lemon juice. Cook, stirring constantly, until the peaches soften and the sauce coats the back of a spoon, 5 to 7 minutes. Remove from the heat and set aside to cool.

TO MAKE THE CRUST: In a 9-inch pie plate, combine the cookie crumbs, brown sugar, and butter and stir until well combined. Use the back of a large spoon to press the crumbs evenly on the bottom and up the sides of the pie pan. Bake in the oven for 10 to 12 minutes or until beginning to brown. Remove from the oven and set aside.

TO MAKE THE SOUR CREAM MIXTURE: In a medium bowl, whisk together the granulated sugar and egg yolks until pale in color, about 3 minutes. Add the sour cream and whisk to combine. Add the tapioca flour and whisk until smooth, then add the vanilla paste and stir to combine.

To assemble, pour the sour cream mixture into the pie crust and arrange the peaches on top. Cover with foil and bake for 35 to 40 minutes, until set but with a slight jiggle in the middle. Uncover and cook for another 5 to 7 minutes or until golden brown. Remove from the oven and let cool completely. Serve immediately or store covered in the refrigerator for up to 3 days.

"Paint the Wall Red" Strawberry Tarts

Here's proof that your favorite small-town chef can turn any nightmare evening into something yummy! This one was inspired by an ill-fated double date. (Also, these tarts are way more practical than a baked Alaska in the shape of Hawaii.)

I was all anxious and awkward, waiting for Jackson to pin down an official date for our first . . . well, um, date, when Lorelai convinced me to run with the wolves and call him myself. (So twenty-first century, right?! She also pulled me off the phone when I started babbling about putting carrots in vases because they were too pretty to eat, thank goodness.)

Well, Lorelai and I ended up on a double date with Jackson and his cousin Rune, and let me just say—that was a great way to rune a perfectly good first date. Not even the anecdote about Lorelai, tarts, and a wall beyond rescue could get him to crack a smile. (We had to paint that wall over to camouflage Lorelai's misadventures in pastry filling.) Bye, Loon!

Yield: 8 tarts
V*

SPECIAL TOOLS:

- Eight 4-inch tart rings (1-inch deep or 4-inch tart pans with removable bottom)

PASTRY:

- 2½ cups all-purpose flour, plus more for the work surface
- 1 teaspoon kosher salt
- 1 tablespoon powdered sugar
- Zest from 1 lime (about 2 teaspoons)
- 1 cup (16 tablespoons) unsalted butter, very cold
- ¼ cup solid vegetable shortening, very cold
- ⅓ cup ice water

Ingredients continue on page 147

TO MAKE THE PASTRY: In a large bowl, combine the flour, salt, powdered sugar, and lime zest. Cut the butter and shortening into tablespoon-size pieces and add them to the flour mixture. Use a pastry cutter or two butter knives to cut the butter and shortening into the flour until all the pieces are pea size or smaller.

Add the ice water a little at a time, using the pastry cutter to work it in, until the dough just holds together. A bit of loose flour is okay. Turn the mixture out onto a lightly floured surface to form into a ball and split in half. Form each half into a disk, wrap in parchment paper, and refrigerate for 30 minutes.

Working with one half at a time, on a lightly floured surface, roll out the dough to about ⅛ inch thick. Cut out 6-inch circles (see notes), fit them down into the tart rings or tart pans, and trim off the excess. Repeat with the second disk of dough until all the tart shells have been made, put them on a rimmed baking sheet, and chill for another 30 minutes.

Preheat the oven to 425°F.

FILLING:

- 4 cups (about 1 pound) whole strawberries, divided
- ½ cup plus 3 tablespoons granulated sugar, divided
- Juice from 1 lime (about 2 tablespoons)
- 6 ounces cream cheese, softened
- 1 egg, separated
- ½ cup crème fraîche
- ¼ cup plus 1 teaspoon cool water, divided
- 2½ teaspoons (1 package) unflavored gelatin

TO MAKE THE FILLING: In a food processor, purée 3 cups of the strawberries. Run the mixture through a chinois or fine-mesh strainer over a bowl, pressing to get as much juice as possible, and discard the solids. You should have about ¾ cup of purée. Stir in ½ cup of the sugar and the lime juice and set aside.

In a medium mixing bowl, combine the remaining 3 tablespoons of sugar, the cream cheese, egg yolk, and crème fraîche. Use a whisk or a hand mixer to blend thoroughly.

Remove the tart shells from the refrigerator, prick liberally all over the bottom with a fork, and bake for 10 minutes or until just beginning to brown.

While baking, in a small bowl, whisk the egg white and 1 teaspoon of the cool water. Remove the tart shells from the oven, brush with the egg white, and bake for 2 minutes more. Remove from the oven again and divide the cream cheese mixture among the tart shells, in a ½-inch layer. Bake again for another 10 to 12 minutes until the crust is golden brown and the cream cheese mixture has puffed and is beginning to brown. Remove from the oven and allow to cool on a wire rack. The cream mixture will deflate.

In a medium saucepan over medium heat, cook the strawberry mixture, stirring occasionally, until it comes to a boil.

While the purée is cooking, in a small bowl, sprinkle the gelatin over the remaining ¼ cup of cool water and allow to bloom.

Boil the purée mixture for 1 minute and then remove it from the heat. Stir in the gelatin mixture until it is completely dissolved. Set aside.

Slice the remaining 1 cup of strawberries, arrange the slices to mostly cover the top of each tart, and then pour the purée mixture over the top of each tart. Cover the sliced berries completely but be careful not to overflow the tart shell. Refrigerate for at least 1 hour or until the gelatin is set. The tart can be served as soon as the gelatin is set but can be stored in the refrigerator for up to 3 days.

NOTES: To cut out the 6-inch pastry rounds, trace a bowl or plate that is the correct size with either a paring knife or pastry wheel.

These tarts can be made vegetarian by using vegetarian gelatin.

The tart shells can be made up to 2 days ahead and stored at room temperature for up to 3 days.

Any extra dough can be used to cut out decorations for the tarts, such as flowers or leaves.

Rocky Road Cookies

Yield: 12 to 14 cookies
V*

- ½ cup (8 tablespoons) unsalted butter, softened (see tip)
- 1 cup packed light or dark brown sugar
- 1 egg, at room temperature
- 2 teaspoons vanilla extract
- 1 cup all-purpose flour
- ⅓ cup Dutch-process cocoa powder, preferably high cocoa fat
- 1½ teaspoons espresso powder
- 1 teaspoon baking powder
- ½ teaspoon salt
- ⅔ cup macadamia nuts (see notes)
- ½ cup mini marshmallows, divided
- ½ cup chocolate chunks or chips

NOTES: You can also use hazelnuts, peanuts, walnuts, or pecans, without the need to crush, in place of the macadamia nuts.

This recipe is vegetarian if using vegetarian marshmallows.

TIP: Take the butter and the egg out of the refrigerator about 45 minutes (30 minutes if your kitchen feels hot or 1 hour if it feels a bit chilly) before you want to use them. The butter will be perfect when it just becomes spreadable.

"Cookies for the Dean and the love and cookies for the love . . ." Young love . . . *sigh* There's nothing more romantic than falling for someone for the first time. No one forgets their first kiss . . . especially not Rory, because it was immediately followed by some accidental shoplifting. (It's okay; eventually all the stolen stuff went back to Doose's.)

These cookies are a big-time crowd-pleaser, bursting with chocolate, marshmallows, and macadamia nuts. They also happen to be Dean Forester's favorite. Lorelai and I knew something had to be up when Rory put some of her own aside to save for him. I mean, Rory, showing patience and restraint when it came to chocolate? Ha! Okay, sure. (Yes, that was snarkasm.)

Here, Dean, these cookies are for you, 'cause you're keen!

Bringing baked goods to a crush means it's serious. But don't forget: You are allowed to sneak a few for yourself, too.

Preheat the oven to 350°F. Line a baking sheet with parchment paper and set aside.

In the bowl of a stand mixer fitted with the paddle attachment or a large bowl if using a hand mixer, beat the butter and brown sugar on medium speed for about 3 minutes, or until fluffy. Scrape down the sides of the bowl and add the egg and vanilla. Beat for another minute on medium-low speed until smooth.

Add the flour, cocoa powder, espresso powder, baking powder, and salt. Beat on low to medium-low speed until just mixed.

Put the macadamia nuts in a resealable plastic bag. Using a heavy pan, pot, or rolling pin, gently crush them into chunks. Stir the macadamia nuts, ¼ cup of the marshmallows, and the chocolate chunks into the batter.

Scoop or spoon the dough into 2 tablespoon–size balls. Gently roll the dough between your palms, tucking in any marshmallows peeking out. Put on the prepared baking sheet about 3 inches apart. Using the heel of your hand, gently press down on each ball to flatten it out slightly. Using the reserved marshmallows, press three into each ball, distributing them evenly and staying away from the edges.

Bake for 10 minutes. Allow the cookies to cool completely on the baking sheet. Plan to make these cookies at least 2 hours or a day ahead of serving, as they are too fragile to eat while still warm. Store in an airtight container, with the layers separated by parchment paper, at room temperature for up to 3 days.

French Fantasy Crème Brûlée

Bonjour, my loves! What's that, you say? You've been volunteered to contribute to the Chilton Bake Sale and you have no idea what to bring? Le stress! Madame Sookie to the rescue!

Here's a fantasy with a foreign accent. So super-extra sexy-sexy. Paris is the city of love, and I dare you not to fall for this silky-smooth crème brûlée. Mais oui, it's also another chance to break out the kitchen torch (I'm fine, it's fine, but hot tip: Watch those bangs when you lean in, eep!)—quelle excitement! For maximum authenticity, make sure that you get in a fight about Cubism while eating this, and definitely do a lot of wild gesticulation. Ooh la la.

Yield: Six 4-ounce servings
V, GF

SPECIAL TOOLS:

- Six 4-ounce ramekins

- 2 cups heavy cream
- 3 teaspoons dried culinary lavender, divided
- 2 teaspoons lemon zest, divided
- ¾ cup granulated sugar, divided
- 2 egg yolks
- 2 whole eggs

Place the ramekins in a large baking dish deep enough to add water. Preheat the oven to 250°F.

In a small saucepan over medium-low heat, combine the cream, 2 teaspoons of the lavender, and 1 teaspoon of the lemon zest, stirring frequently, until just beginning to simmer. Remove from the heat and allow to steep for 5 minutes.

In a medium heatproof bowl, combine ½ cup of the sugar, the egg yolks, and whole eggs and stir gently until just combined. Set aside.

After the cream mixture has finished steeping, put it back on the stove over medium-low heat and cook until just about to simmer. Gently stir the cream mixture into the egg mixture until well combined. Strain through a fine-mesh strainer into a bowl or large measuring cup. Pour into the ramekins, coming just up to the lip.

Put the baking dish in the oven and fill with warm water until three-quarters of the way up the sides of the ramekins. Bake for 1 to 1½ hours or until set but with a slight jiggle in the middle.

While the crème brûlées are baking, in a small airtight container, combine the remaining ¼ cup of sugar, remaining 1 teaspoon of lavender, and remaining 1 teaspoon of lemon zest. Shake thoroughly to combine.

Using tongs or an oven mitt, remove the ramekins from the water bath and allow to cool to room temperature. Cover each ramekin tightly with plastic wrap and refrigerate for a minimum of 8 hours or up to 2 days.

When ready to serve, set the oven to broil. Press the sugar mixture through a fine-mesh strainer over a bowl and discard the solids. Sprinkle about 2 teaspoons of the sugar mixture evenly across the surface of each crème brûlée. Caramelize the sugar under the broiler, watching carefully, for about 1 minute, or use a kitchen torch to brûlée the top of each dessert.

Remind Michel—Paw-Paw's dry cleaning (?) to be dropped off Thurs.
—Lorelai

Yield: 8 servings
V

SPECIAL TOOLS:

- 9-inch pie plate
- Star- and heart-shaped cookie cutters (optional)

PASTRY:

- 2½ cups all-purpose flour, plus more for the work surface
- 1 teaspoon kosher salt
- 2 teaspoons powdered sugar
- 1 teaspoon ground ginger
- ½ cup (8 tablespoons) unsalted butter, very cold
- ¼ cup vegetable shortening, very cold
- ⅓ cup ice water
- 2 tablespoons cream, for glazing

FILLING:

- 6 cups fresh blackberries
- 1 teaspoon freshly grated ginger
- ¾ cup granulated sugar, plus more for dusting
- ¼ cup tapioca starch
- 2 tablespoons unsalted butter, cut into small pieces
- Purple sanding sugar, for decorating (optional)

- Whipped cream or vanilla ice cream, for serving (optional)

Stars Hollow Says Goodbye Blackberry Pie

"Wow, two pies" had nothing to do with my amazing baking skills, unfortunately. It was what Lorelai said to Jess and Luke the night we all first met Jess, when he came to Stars Hollow to live with Luke. She meant for smashing in faces, 'cause of rudeness (Jess's, duh).

Jess stayed pretty unflappable, which was super annoying, because I for one would have paid good money to see that smug little jerk . . . well, flap a little bit. (At least he didn't tie anyone to a chair or anything like that. Back when I first got pregnant, I assumed that's what all kids did. Even smug teenaged kids.)

"Two pies" here refers to two of the different pies I made for Rory's farewell party. Fresh, ripe berries will make this one soar. Bon voyage, Rory! Remember—home is where the pie(s) are! You can make this one even if no one's going anywhere; I won't tell.

TO MAKE THE PASTRY: In a large mixing bowl, combine the flour, salt, powdered sugar, and ginger. Cut the butter and shortening into tablespoon-size pieces and add them to the flour mixture. Use a pastry cutter or two butter knives to cut the butter and shortening into the flour until all the pieces are pea size.

Add the ice water a little at a time, using the pastry cutter to work it in, until the dough just holds together. A bit of loose flour is okay. Turn the mixture out onto a lightly floured surface to form into a ball and split in half. Roll out one half to ⅛ inch thick, large enough to fit your pie plate with a little overhang. Fit it into the pie plate, trim the excess close to the edge, and crimp as desired. Roll the second piece out on a silicone baking mat or parchment paper and slide onto a baking sheet. Refrigerate the pie plate and dough for 30 minutes.

Fifteen minutes into the pastry rest, preheat the oven to 450°F.

TO MAKE THE FILLING: In a large bowl, mix the blackberries and ginger. Sprinkle the granulated sugar and tapioca starch over the berries and stir to combine. Allow to rest for 15 minutes.

Remove the rolled-out pastry from the refrigerator and use the star cookie cutter to cut out as many stars as you can and one heart, if using. Remove the pie pan from the refrigerator and fill with the berry mixture. Scatter the butter over the top. Brush cream over the entire edge of the crust. Use the stars and the heart to create a lattice top for the pie, making sure that each star touches the edge at least once. Brush all the pieces with more cream. Sprinkle each star with purple sanding sugar, if using, or regular sugar. If not using cookie cutters, top the pie with a top crust, and cut three vents in the middle.

Bake the pie for 10 minutes on the top rack and then reduce the temperature to 350°F. Slip a rimmed baking sheet on the rack under the pie to catch any drips. Bake for 35 to 40 minutes or until the pastry is golden brown and the fruit is bubbly. If the crust is getting too brown before the fruit is bubbling, cover the crust lightly with foil.

Allow to cool to room temperature before serving. The pie can be stored at room temperature for 3 days. Serve with whipped cream or vanilla ice cream.

Muffin Bottom Meringue and Ice-Cream Pie

Everyone knows the top is the best part of the muffin. Well, everyone who's right about the best part of muffins, that is. (Even if it's not *your* thing—okay, weirdo—I've baked enough muffin tops that coming up with a way to use up the leftover muffins was a thing.

What can I say? A surprise morning delivery of coffee and a basket of fresh-baked muffin tops *happens* to be the best way to say, "You're my best friend and you're very, very pretty, and I love you, and also would you mind pretty please watching my children today so my husband and I can go skiing?" (Or, I guess it could say whatever *you* need it to say, in a pinch.) The muffin top bribe system works, so obviously I know what I'm doing. Your muffin mileage may vary.

Yield: 6 mini pies
V

SPECIAL TOOLS:

- 2-inch ice-cream scoop
- Six 4-ounce ramekins
- Kitchen torch

- About ½ quart Cider Ice Cream (page 157) or ice cream of choice
- 6 Apple-Cinnamon Walnut or Double-Chocolate Chip Muffin bottoms (page 40)
- 1 tablespoon meringue powder
- ½ cup granulated sugar
- ¼ cup cool water

OPTIONAL FLAVORINGS:

- ½ teaspoon ground cinnamon and ½ teaspoon vanilla paste (for the Apple-Cinnamon Walnut Muffin version)
- ½ teaspoon espresso powder and 1 teaspoon vanilla paste (for the Double-Chocolate Chip Muffin version)

Cover a baking sheet with parchment paper. Use the ice-cream scoop to scoop out six scoops of ice cream, put them on the prepared baking sheet, and freeze for at least 2 hours or up to overnight (see notes).

Preheat the oven to 350°F. Take each muffin bottom and press them into the bottom of each ramekin. Bake for 12 to 15 minutes or until just starting to toast. Remove from the oven and set aside.

Fit a large heatproof mixing bowl or the bowl of a stand mixer into a large pot. Fill the pot with water so that it goes about halfway up the sides of the bowl. Put the pot on the stove over medium-high heat and whisk the meringue powder, sugar, and water. Continue to whisk until the mixture is smooth and viscous and you can't feel any sugar granules when rubbed between your fingers, 5 to 7 minutes.

Remove from the heat, add the cinnamon or espresso powder, and use a hand mixer to beat on high speed until stiff peaks form and the sides of the bowl feel cool, up to 20 minutes. Add the vanilla paste and beat on medium speed until just incorporated. This is best used right away, but it can be covered and stored at room temperature for up to 3 hours.

To assemble, place an ice-cream scoop onto each muffin bottom. Starting at the top, spread a scant ½ cup of meringue onto the ice cream, making sure to completely cover the ice cream and seal it against the edges of the ramekin. Use the torch to generously brown the meringue. Serve immediately.

NOTES: The longer the ice-cream scoops pre-freeze, the easier they will be to work with, so preparing them the day before is a great way to set up for success.

This recipe is *not* a candidate for the broiler to toast the meringue because the broiler will melt both the meringue and the ice cream.

ughters of the American Revolution
Annual Luncheon
Menu
Brie Wheel with
Lavender Honey and
Bourbon-Sugared Pecans
Mushroom Soup
Stuffed Pork Cho
with Madera Poache
Fig, Arugula, and P
Chocolate A
Mousse

Chocolate Amaretto Mousse Cake (In the Shape of a G)

Unlike that creepy neighbor with the Tannis root, this is a dessert that announces itself unequivocally. No sneaking up on you whatsoever, no sirree, Bob. (Also, no undertaste, obviously, and no weird cult conspiring to knock you up with the spawn of Satan. So that's good.)

Once we got past all the classic horror film jokes (If you don't understand them, ask Dean!), this one was smooth sailing all the way. Mousse—not "mouse," another one for the insiders—is basically pudding but fancier, making it perfectamundo for a huge fancy dinner in honor of the third Lorelai Gilmore. (Or, I guess she's actually the first, because we're talking about Richard's mother here.)

This dessert was the cap to a twelve-course meal, each course with its own wine pairing. Shape your mousse-filled meringues into the letter of your preference. It's work, but it's worth the extra touch, in my opinion.

Yield: 4 cakes
V, GF

SPECIAL TOOLS:

- 3 pastry bags
- Large, round pastry bag tip (such as 807)
- 2 different-size open or closed star pastry bag tips

CHOCOLATE CRÉMEUX:

- 6 ounces bittersweet chocolate, chopped
- 8 ounces milk chocolate, chopped
- 2 tablespoons amaretto
- 1 tablespoon vanilla extract
- 4 egg yolks (reserve the whites for the macarons)
- ¼ cup granulated sugar
- 1 cup whole milk
- 1 cup heavy cream

Ingredients continue on page 156

TO MAKE THE CHOCOLATE CRÉMEUX: Put each type of chocolate in separate, 2-cup (or larger), heatproof measuring cups or bowls. Add the amaretto to the bittersweet chocolate and the vanilla to the milk chocolate and set aside.

In a medium bowl, whisk together the egg yolks and granulated sugar until thick and pale, about 3 minutes. Set aside.

In a heavy-bottomed saucepan over medium heat, combine the milk and cream and cook, stirring frequently, until the mixture begins to steam, 5 to 7 minutes. Remove the pan from the heat and slowly ladle about one-third of the milk mixture into the eggs, whisking quickly and constantly. This will temper the eggs so they don't scramble. Add the egg mixture back to the saucepan with the remaining milk mixture and return to the stove over medium-low heat.

Continue to cook the mixture, using a rubber spatula to stir almost constantly and scrape the bottom and creases of the pan, until the mixture thickens. The mixture should be thick enough to fully coat the back of the spatula (this can take up to 30 minutes).

Once the mixture has thickened, remove from the heat, split it evenly between the two bowls of chocolate, and let stand for 5 minutes. After 5 minutes, stir each mixture until completely smooth. Cover with plastic wrap touching the surface of the crémeux and refrigerate for at least 4 hours or preferably overnight. This can be made up to 3 days ahead.

Better yet, why not just ask Pennilyn Lott to make them?!
—Emily

MACARONS:

- 1 cup fine, blanched almond flour
- 6 tablespoons cocoa powder
- 2 cups powdered sugar
- 4 egg whites
- ⅛ teaspoon cream of tartar
- ½ cup superfine sugar
- 1 teaspoon vanilla extract
- 1 teaspoon amaretto

ASSEMBLY:

- ½ cup white chocolate chips
- ½ cup semi-sweet chocolate chips
- Gold candy pearls, for garnish

NOTE: These desserts can be assembled up to 24 hours in advance. You can also pipe the macaron in another letter or even simple shapes such as circles, hearts, or leaves to suit your occasion.

TO MAKE THE MACARONS: In the bowl of a food processor, pulse the almond flour, cocoa powder, and powdered sugar for about 1 minute, stopping and then pulsing again as necessary to combine. Sift over a large bowl twice. After two siftings, you may discard up to 1 teaspoon of solids.

In the bowl of a stand mixer fitted with a whisk attachment or a large mixing bowl if using a hand mixer (although this will take a long time if not using a stand mixer), combine the egg whites and cream of tartar. Whisk on high speed until soft peaks form. With the mixer running, slowly sprinkle in the superfine sugar and continue to whisk until stiff peaks form. The meringue should hold a point when the whisk is pulled away from it.

Add the meringue all at once to the almond flour mixture along with the vanilla and amaretto and use a rubber spatula to pull the meringue through the almond mixture (this process is called macaronage). The mixture should be fully combined and fall away from the spatula in a slow ribbon. Do not overmix.

Preheat the oven to 350°F and line four baking sheets with parchment paper. Fit a pastry bag with the tip and fill with the meringue.

Pipe two Gs onto two baking sheets, tap the sheets gently to remove air bubbles, and let rest for 15 minutes. Bake for 10 to 12 minutes or until crisp and firm. While the first set of Gs is baking, pipe the remaining four onto the other two baking sheets. Remove the first baking sheets from the oven and allow to cool completely on the baking sheet.

Use a large spatula to remove the macarons from the baking sheet and store between layers of parchment paper in an airtight container for up to 3 days.

TO ASSEMBLE: In a heatproof bowl, microwave the white chocolate chips in 20-second increments, stirring in between each one. Stir until smooth. Choose the four best Gs as tops and set onto a baking sheet (they can be quite close together). Use a whisk to drizzle the chocolate over the macarons, creating a striped effect, and set aside for 5 minutes or until set.

Repeat the process followed for the white chocolate chips with the semi-sweet chocolate chips.

Fit the other two pastry bags with the other two pastry tips and fill with the crémeux.

Place the bottom macarons on a baking sheet and pipe the crémeux onto each one, alternating between the two flavors and covering the entire surface edge to edge. Gently lift the tops, breaking away chocolate strands from the center of each G. Gently place a top on each crémeux-covered base, pressing only slightly to attach.

Pipe three stars at the bottom left of each G and sprinkle with gold pearls, if using. Refrigerate until serving.

Cider Ice Cream

I scream, you scream, we all scream, sure—that's how the saying goes, after all . . .

But no one screams quite as loudly as Luke when Taylor's cooking up a scheme—like a hay bale maze that just so happens to pin Luke and all his customers inside the diner.

Or the time Taylor decided Stars Hollow needed a spot for old-fashioned fountain drinks like root beer floats and egg creams (which Lorelai thought sounded icky, until she learned about the ice-cream part). Enter the soda shoppe, extra "P-E" and all—no matter how much Luke stomped and stormed.

Because as much as he can be a tad annoying (there's a reason Jackson ran for town selectman, and it wasn't because he actually wanted to be town selectman), Taylor was right—ice cream makes everything better (like egg creams). This one pairs well with Muffin Bottom Meringue and Ice-Cream Pie (page 152); just saying.

Yield: About 1½ quarts
V, GF

- 2 cups unfiltered apple juice
- 1 cinnamon stick
- 1 teaspoon whole allspice
- 1 teaspoon whole cloves
- One 14-ounce can sweetened condensed milk
- 2½ cups heavy cream

In a heavy-bottomed saucepan over medium-high heat, combine the apple juice, cinnamon, allspice, and cloves. Bring to a boil, then reduce the heat to low. Simmer the apple juice between 25 to 35 minutes or until reduced by half. Using your hood fan can help speed up this process a bit. Once the juice has reduced, pour it through a strainer into a heatproof container and discard the spices. Refrigerate and allow to cool completely.

In a medium bowl, whisk the sweetened condensed milk and reduced apple juice until thoroughly combined. In the bowl of a stand mixer or a large mixing bowl if using a hand mixer, whip the cream on high speed until stiff peaks form. Turn the mixer to low speed and slowly drizzle in the condensed milk mixture. When all the milk mixture has been completely incorporated, put in an airtight container and freeze overnight before serving.

Zabaglione with Berries and Pine Nut Meringue Cookies

Mamma mia! (Especially when that mamma is Emily Gilmore, and she's trying to hijack your post-Europe, pre-Yale biscotti night.) This recipe is another entry from the annals of the Chilton Bake Sale. This is what happens when Lorelai's ordered to get more involved—I get the urge to whisk. I need to whisk. I yearn for it, crave it! I just can't help myself! The way Lorelai feels about coffee? That's how I feel about a good old-fashioned hand whisk. (Silver lining? I'm a total ringer in an arm-wrestling match. Any challengers?)

This is a simple recipe for a zabaglione, a traditional Italian custard. (It's pronounced "zuh-buh-glee-OWN"—as in, hands off mine, no sharing, go get your own.) A few fresh, standout ingredients are key. Ripe summer berries and pine nut meringue cookies round everything out. What did I say about getting (or making?) your own?!

Take the zabaglione—you'll leave the cannoli, I promise. Unlike Lorelai and Rory while they were traipsing around Europe all summer while I was stranded with my big, huge pregnant belly, the cannoli won't be missed.

Yield: 6 servings
V, GF*

SPECIAL TOOL:

- Pastry bag with large star or round tip

PINE NUT MERINGUE COOKIES:

- 1½ cups raw pine nuts (see notes)
- 3 large egg whites, at room temperature (reserve the yolks for the zabaglione) (see tip)
- ¼ teaspoon cream of tartar
- ⅛ teaspoon kosher salt
- 1 cup granulated sugar
- ¼ teaspoon almond extract

ZABAGLIONE:

- 6 large egg yolks, at room temperature
- ⅓ cup granulated sugar
- ⅓ cup Pineapple-Infused Vodka (page 136) or Marsala
- Pinch of salt

- 1 pound berries, single variety or mixed, slicing the strawberries if using

TO MAKE THE PINE NUT MERINGUE COOKIES: Preheat the oven to 350°F.

Toast the pine nuts on a rimmed baking sheet, shaking the pan once or twice while baking, until just golden, 3 to 4 minutes. Allow to cool completely. Once cool, using a chef's knife, coarsely chop the pine nuts and set aside. Depending on the size of your cutting board, this may be easier in batches (see notes).

Reduce the oven temperature to 300°F. Line a large baking sheet with parchment paper. Set up your pastry bag with a large star or round tip.

In the bowl of a stand mixer or a large mixing bowl if using a hand mixer, beat the egg whites using a whisk attachment or hand mixer on low speed for 3 minutes, or until the entire surface is covered in tiny bubbles. Add the cream of tartar and salt and increase the speed to medium. Once soft peaks appear, sprinkle the sugar in 1 tablespoon at a time. Increase the speed to high and continue beating until it reaches a thick marshmallowy consistency and holds stiff peaks, about 5 minutes, drizzling in the almond extract at the very end. Using a rubber spatula, gently fold in the pine nuts until just incorporated. Do not overmix.

Gently spoon the meringue into the prepared pastry bag. Pipe 2-inch-long bars onto the prepared baking sheet, bringing the tip back toward the middle of the cookie as you pull up and spacing the bars about 1½ inches apart. Alternatively, drop heaping teaspoonfuls onto the prepared baking sheet. Bake until lightly brown, 15 to 18 minutes. Remove from the oven and set the baking pan on a wire rack to cool for 2 hours. Store at room temperature in an airtight container, layered with parchment paper, for up to 5 days.

TO MAKE THE ZABAGLIONE: Fill a medium saucepan with 1 inch of water and bring to a very gentle simmer over medium heat. Reduce the heat to low. Find a large heatproof glass, stainless steel, or copper bowl that sits snugly on your saucepan without the bottom touching the water but do not place in the pan yet. In the bowl, whisk the egg yolks and sugar until smooth. Whisk in the vodka until just foamy.

Put the bowl over the saucepan. Whisk immediately, using a potholder to hold the bowl in place with your other hand. Whisk constantly until it begins to thicken, leaving ribbons as you let the mixture fall off the whisk, 7 to 10 minutes. Remove from the heat and set on a folded kitchen towel to prevent the bowl from sliding. Add the salt and continue to whisk until further thickened and cooled to room temperature, about 5 more minutes.

If serving immediately, divide the fruit among six serving glasses. Top with the zabaglione and serve with one or two pine nut cookies, either on the side or crumbled on top. If making ahead, put the zabaglione in an airtight container in the refrigerator for up to 24 hours before assembling.

TIP: Separate your eggs one at a time, collecting the whites in a small bowl before adding to the mixing bowl, to be sure you don't have any yolk. Yolk in your whites will make it impossible to properly whip your meringue.

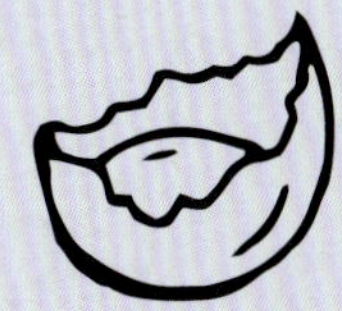

NOTES: Do not double the cookie recipe. The batter deflates quickly, so make sure you are ready to pipe and bake immediately after making the batter.

Do not use a food processor to chop the pine nuts. Doing so will release too much oil from the pine nuts, leaving you with flatter cookies.

This recipe is gluten free if gluten-free vodka is used in the Pineapple-Infused Vodka.

Yield: 28 to 32 servings

SPECIAL TOOLS:

- Half-sheet pan (about 11½ by 16½ inches)
- Cake strips (optional)
- Candy thermometer

MARSHMALLOWS:

- 3 tablespoons meringue powder
- 1⅓ cups cool water, divided
- 2 envelopes (5 teaspoons) unflavored gelatin
- ⅓ cup honey
- 1 cup granulated sugar
- ⅛ teaspoon salt
- ½ cup powdered sugar
- ½ cup cornstarch

Ingredients continue on page 162

Dark Chocolate S'mores Wedding Cake

One bite of this cake and everyone will be asking for s'more! This recipe is literally a dream come true—it came to me in a dream, and then I made it come true. Ha!

As Best Friend of the Bride (BFOTB), I cycled through a lot of trial wedding cakes. A lot. (RIP, Claude and co.) This was the only cake to make it to prime time (sadly, not for Luke and Lorelai). It was still a huge hit—that homemade toffee!

And unlike Taylor, I had total faith that those two would get it together to get married well before classic rock bands from the '60s reunited (not only because of how some of them are gone). When I found that cake topper at that flea market, I just knew. The groom had Luke's butt! Luke's butt! Okay, we should probably stop now, he's getting annoyed.

TO MAKE THE MARSHMALLOWS: In the bowl of a stand mixer fitted with a whisk attachment, combine the meringue powder and ½ cup of the water. Whisk on low speed until frothy, then turn the mixer off.

Pour ½ cup of water into a small bowl and sprinkle with the gelatin. Set aside to bloom.

In a heavy-bottomed saucepan fitted with a candy thermometer, combine the remaining ⅓ cup of water, the honey, and granulated sugar. Over medium-high heat, cook the syrup, without stirring, until the thermometer reaches 210°F. At this time, add the salt to the mixer, turn it to high speed, and whisk until stiff peaks form.

When the syrup temperature reaches 245°F, remove it from the heat. Turn the mixer off, add about one-third of the syrup, being careful not to spill it on the whisk, and mix on high speed for 15 seconds. Repeat until all the syrup has been added to the mixer. Continue to whisk the mixture on high speed. Add the gelatin mixture to the saucepan and use the residual heat to melt the gelatin. Return the pan to the stove over low heat if a bit more heat is needed. Once the gelatin is melted, turn the mixer off, add the gelatin all at once, turn the mixer back to high speed, and continue to whisk until the bowl is completely cool to the touch.

GRAHAM CRACKER TOFFEE:

- 3 sleeves graham crackers (about 14 ounces), divided
- 1¼ cups (20 tablespoons) unsalted butter
- 1½ teaspoons kosher salt
- 1 cup packed dark brown sugar
- 2 cups semisweet chocolate chips (12 ounces)

CAKE:

- 3 cups granulated sugar
- 2⅔ cups all-purpose flour
- 1⅓ cups cocoa powder
- 1 teaspoon salt
- 2½ teaspoons baking powder
- 2½ teaspoons baking soda
- 4 eggs
- 1 cup whole milk
- 1 tablespoon vanilla extract
- 1½ cups (24 tablespoons) salted butter, melted
- 1¼ cups boiling water

Ingredients continue on page 163

While the marshmallow is cooling, prepare the coating by whisking the powdered sugar and cornstarch together in a small bowl. Use a fine sifter to coat the surface of a rimmed baking sheet entirely with the mixture, leaving no bare patches. When the marshmallow is completely cool, use an offset spatula to spread the marshmallow into an even layer on the prepared baking sheet. Let dry, uncovered, in a cool dry place overnight. Cover the remaining coating powder and store at room temperature (you will use it multiple times in the process).

When ready to cut, dust the entire top of the marshmallow sheet with some of the coating powder. You can cut the marshmallows into any size and shape using kitchen shears, a pizza wheel, or cookie cutters like the hearts for this cake. Coat each cut piece by tossing it in the bowl with the coating and shaking off the excess.

These marshmallows can be stored in an airtight container for up to 1 week.

TO MAKE THE GRAHAM CRACKER TOFFEE: Preheat the oven to 350°F. Line a half-sheet pan with foil, leaving some hanging over each short end, then line the foil with parchment paper, leaving ends again. Lay out the graham crackers on the parchment paper so that they cover the entire sheet pan and fit tightly. Leave as many as you can whole but break in half or quarters as needed to fill the space.

In a medium heavy-bottomed saucepan over medium-high heat, melt the butter. Once the butter is melted, add the salt and brown sugar and bring to a boil. Once the mixture boils, reduce the heat to medium-low and simmer, stirring constantly. Continue to cook until all the sugar is dissolved and the mixture thickens slightly, 5 to 7 minutes. Pour the mixture over the graham crackers and use an offset spatula to spread it evenly. Bake for 5 to 7 minutes or until the toffee is bubbling all over. Remove it from the oven, and once it stops bubbling, sprinkle with the chocolate chips and let stand for 5 minutes. Once melted, use a clean offset spatula to spread the chocolate in an even layer. Allow to cool completely (you can do this at room temperature or refrigerate for 10 to 15 minutes). Once the chocolate is set, break the toffee into bark pieces and crumble about half of it. Store the crumbles and bark in separate airtight containers until needed. This can be made up to 5 days in advance.

TO MAKE THE CAKE: Preheat the oven to 350°F. Line three 8-inch round cake pans and two 6-inch round cake pans with rounds of parchment paper and wrap with cake strips, if using (see notes).

Over the bowl of a stand mixer or a large mixing bowl if using a hand mixer, sift together the granulated sugar, flour, cocoa, salt, baking powder, and baking soda. Using a whisk attachment or hand mixer, blend briefly on low speed.

In a separate medium mixing bowl, whisk together the eggs, milk, vanilla, and melted butter until well combined. Add the egg mixture to the flour mixture and mix on low speed for 3 minutes. Slowly add the boiling water and mix on low speed until combined. Make sure to scrape the bottom of the bowl, as the batter will be very thin.

Fill each 8-inch pan with 2 cups of the batter and each 6-inch pan with 1 cup of the batter. Bake for 15 to 20 minutes or until a cake tester comes out clean. Allow the cakes to cool in the pan for 15 minutes. After 15 minutes, run an offset spatula gently around the edge of each cake and turn them out onto wire racks to cool completely.

Either use immediately or wrap each layer in parchment paper and then in plastic wrap and refrigerate for up to 3 days or freeze for up to 3 weeks. The cake does not have to be defrosted for assembly but should be allowed to come to room temperature for 30 minutes before serving.

TO MAKE THE BROWN SUGAR FROSTING: In the bowl of a stand mixer fitted with a whisk attachment, combine the egg whites and salt but do not mix yet.

In a heavy-bottomed saucepan fitted with a candy thermometer over medium-high heat, stir together the water and brown sugar and bring to a boil. When the sugar begins to boil, start mixing the egg whites on medium-high speed until frothy. Add the lemon juice and mix again on medium-high speed until soft peaks form. Stop the mixer.

Grease a 2-cup heatproof measuring cup with butter. Continue to boil the sugar until the temperature reaches between 238°F and 242°F. Remove from the heat and pour into the greased measuring cup. Slowly add the sugar syrup to the egg whites in small amounts at a time, whisking after each addition. When all the syrup is added, beat the mixture on high speed until the meringue is completely cool (the outside of the bowl should be completely cool to the touch).

Add the butter one piece at a time, beating on medium speed after each addition. Add the vanilla and beat again on medium speed until light and fluffy, 1 to 2 minutes.

TO MAKE THE MARSHMALLOW FILLING: Line a rimmed baking sheet with parchment paper. Lay out the marshmallow in a single layer on the prepared baking sheet and place under the broiler for 30 seconds to 1 minute or until the marshmallows are golden brown in most places and dark brown in some. Watch carefully. Remove the marshmallows from the oven and let them cool completely. Put the frosting in a large mixing bowl. Use a spatula to scrape the marshmallow off the baking sheet and fold it into the frosting. Continue to stir, about a minute, until the marshmallow has evenly dispersed.

TO ASSEMBLE THE CAKE: Put an 8-inch cake layer on a cake board or serving plate and spread 1 cup of the marshmallow filling evenly across it. Cover the filling with 1 cup of the crushed graham cracker toffee and repeat with the second 8-inch layer. Place the third 8-inch layer on top and use the brown sugar frosting to lightly crumb-coat the entire cake, filling in the gaps between the layers. Refrigerate the cake for 15 minutes.

BROWN SUGAR FROSTING:

- 9 egg whites
- ½ teaspoon salt
- ¾ cup water
- 3 cups packed light brown sugar
- 1½ teaspoons lemon juice
- 4½ cups unsalted (72 tablespoons) butter, plus more for greasing
- 1 tablespoon vanilla extract

MARSHMALLOW FILLING:

- 6 cups Marshmallow scraps (10 ounces)
- 3 cups Brown Sugar Frosting

Ingredients continue on page 164

GANACHE:

- 2 cups bittersweet chocolate chips (or 12 ounces bittersweet chocolate, chopped)
- 1 cup heavy cream
- 1 tablespoon honey

While the 8-inch cake is in the refrigerator, work with the 6-inch layers. Put one of the layers on a cake board about 1 inch smaller than the cake. Use about ½ cup of the marshmallow filling to cover the top of this layer and top with ½ cup of the crushed toffee. Place the second layer on top and use the brown sugar frosting to crumb-coat the entire cake. Refrigerate for 15 minutes.

Frost both the 8-inch and 6-inch layers completely with brown sugar frosting and refrigerate for 30 minutes.

TO MAKE THE GANACHE: While the cakes are refrigerating, microwave the chocolate chips and cream in a microwave-safe measuring cup or bowl for 1 minute and allow to stand for 5 minutes. Stir until completely smooth and then stir in the honey. Set aside.

After the cakes have been in the refrigerator for 30 minutes, pour the ganache over each cake, just covering the tops, and, using the end of an offset spatula, press some of the ganache toward the edges and allow it to drip decoratively down the sides. Refrigerate until ready to set up and serve.

Stack the 6-inch cake on top of the 8-inch cake, centering it. Decorate with the small heart-shaped marshmallows to create borders for each cake. Use some graham-cracker-bark pieces and large hearts to make a topper. The top hearts can be lightly toasted with a kitchen torch, if desired. The completely assembled cake can sit out for up to 3 hours, as long as it is a cool place out of direct sunlight.

NOTES: Just lining the bottom of the pans with parchment and not greasing the whole cake pan allows the batter to climb to its maximum height. Cake strips help prevent domes and result in very level cakes. If you don't use cake strips, you will need to trim the domes off your cakes before assembly.

It is not recommended to use a hand mixer with the marshmallow or frosting recipes. The syrups are very hot, and the stability of a stand mixer ensures that you will not spill or splash hot syrup on yourself.

Sookie!

Love the cookbook! I'd say it's your masterpiece, but that may have been Clyde. Or the French toast. Or, oh my god, that peach sauce (though I'm glad you talked me out of bathing in it). Except now I'm leaving out the savory stuff, like Chicken Taquito Blinis with Avocado Crema, or Pasta à la Sookie, or the Steak Haché with Peppercorn Sauce . . .

Forget it, I can't pick just one! I mean, the mom from that World War II movie who had to choose between her kids didn't have it so hard. (Cakes don't have legs! Who will rescue the cakes from an imaginary burning building if not us?)

But I digress. Congratulations, this is amazing! We both know I'll never cook from it, but it's going to be on display (and on sale) at the inn. I'm guessing your editor might have a few tiny notes for you before it's ready for publication?

But—copper boom!—when it's good to go, you can bet I'll be there!

XO,

Lorelai

Suggested Menus

Bracebridge Dinner

- ☐ Bracebridge Dinner Butternut Squash Soup (page 59)
- ☐ Trout Salad with Lemon-Chive Vinaigrette (page 77)
- ☐ Bracebridge Dinner Peacock Pie (page 111)
- ☐ Apple Chutney (page 17)
- ☐ Baron of Beef with Sauce Diane (page 118)
- ☐ Plum Pudding with Hard Sauce (page 140)
- ☐ Wassail (page 123)

Brunch

- ☐ Muffin Tops Two Ways (page 40)
- ☐ Luke's Diner Cajun Eggs Benedict (page 44)
- ☐ Belgian Waffles with Famous Peach Sauce (page 34)
- ☐ Shirred Eggs with Chive (page 37)
- ☐ "Coffee! Coffee! Coffee!" Martini (page 132)
- ☐ Bacon-Infused Vodka Bloody Mary (page 130)

Can't go wrong with my Famous Peach Sauce!

DAR-Style Elegant Lunch

- ☐ "Enscotched" Cocktail (page 124)
- ☐ Brie Wheel with Lavender Honey and Bourbon-Candied Pecans (page 62)
- ☐ Emily's "This Is Delicious" Mushroom Soup (page 68)
- ☐ Pork Chops with Madeira-Poached Pears (page 99)
- ☐ Fig, Prosciutto, and Burrata Salad (page 82)
- ☐ Chocolate Amaretto Mousse Cake (In the Shape of a G) (page 155)

High Tea

- Ginger Fizz (page 129)
- Currant and Spice Scones (page 38)
- Thank-You Jam (page 23)
- Mini Orange-Glazed Biscuit Sandwiches (page 89)
- "Paint the Wall Red" Strawberry Tarts (page 145)

Romantic Dinner

- ☐ Walnut Arugula Gorgonzola Crostini (page 64)
- ☐ Lamb Chops and Sicilian Olive Gremolata (page 96)
- ☐ Warm Potato and Chorizo Salad (page 87)
- ☐ Roasted Asparagus with Tomatoes and Parmesan Cheese (page 81)
- ☐ Raspberry Mousse with Candied Kumquats and Kumquat Gelée (page 142)
- ☐ Wine

Comfort Food Night In

- ☐ Chocolate Chocolate Chip Milkshake (page 134)
- ☐ Chicken Taquito Blinis with Avocado Crema (page 53)
- ☐ Mini "Bratwursts" (page 56)
- ☐ Slice of Dark Chocolate S'mores Wedding Cake (page 160)
- ☐ Rocky Road Cookies (page 148)
- ☐ Muffin Tops Two Ways (page 40)
- ☐ Muffin Bottom Meringue and Ice-Cream Pie (page 152)
- ☐ Ennui / Off-oui, "Oh, Hey, I'm Cured" Cocktail (page 136)
- ☐ The Original Onion Dip (page 55)

Dietary Considerations

Chapter One: The Pantry

Homemade Brioche Bread. V

"Bid on a Basket" Pineapple-Cranberry Chutney. . . . . . . V, V+, GF

Famous Peach Sauce . . . . V, V+, GF

Brandied Cherries. . . . . V, V+, GF

Apple Chutney. . . . . V, V+, GF

Infused Vinegars & Olive Oils:

- Blackberry-Rosemary Vinegar. . . . . V, GF
- Meyer Lemon-Infused Vinegar. . . . . V, GF
- Spice-Infused Olive Oils . . . . V, V+, GF

Pickled Radish Roses. . . . . V, V+, GF

Thank-You Jam. . . . . V, GF

Tomato Sauce: "Godfather It Up" Puttanesca. . . . . V+*, GF*

Quick Puff Pastry V

Lemon-Chive Vinaigrette . . . . V+*, GF

Chapter Two: Breakfast

"I Have My Standards" Omelets. . . . . GF

Healthy (Boring) Egg-White Omelet . . V, GF

Blueberry-Lemon Pancakes. V

Belgium Waffles with Famous Peach Sauce V

Shirred Eggs with Chive . . . . V, GF*

Currant and Spice Scones V

Muffin Tops Two Ways. V

Orange-Glazed Muffins with Warm Cinnamon Butter V

Luke's Diner Cajun Eggs Benedict

Caramelized Hazelnut Brioche French Toast V

Chapter Three: Starters

Chicken Taquito Blinis with Avocado Crema

The Original Onion Dip . . . . V, GF

Mini "Bratwursts"

Bracebridge Dinner Butternut Squash Soup. . . . . V, V+*, GF

Rory's Birthday Angel Wings with Sweet Chile Dipping Sauce . . . . GF*

Brie Wheel with Lavender Honey and Bourbon-Candied Pecans . . . . . . GF

Walnut Arugula Gorgonzola Crostini . . GF*

Mourning Mock Turtle Soup

"The Lettuce Is Dry" BLT Soup

Emily's "This Is Delicious" Mushroom Soup . . . . V*, GF*

Chapter Four: Sandwiches, Salads & Sides

Jackson's Vegetables Carpaccio. . . . . V, V+, GF

Not Jackson's Vegetables Ratatouille. . . . . V, V+, GF

Trout Salad with Lemon-Chive Vinaigrette. . . . . GF

Hothouse Tomato Salad with Fresh Herbs. . . . . V, V+, GF

Roasted Asparagus with Tomatoes and Parmesan Cheese. . . . . V*, GF

Late-Summer Salads:

- Fig, Prosciutto, and Burrata Salad. . GF
- Watermelon, Peach, and Feta with Mint Salad . . . . GF

Couscous Salad with Garden Vegetables. . . . . V, V+, GF*

Warm Potato and Chorizo Salad . . . . GF

Mini Orange-Glazed Biscuit Sandwiches

Baked Corned Beef Brisket Sandwiches on Rye . . . . GF*

Sweet Potato Biscuit Sandwiches

V: Vegetarian	V+*: Easily made vegan
V*: Easily made vegetarian	GF: Gluten free
V+: Vegan	GF*: Easily made gluten free

Chapter Five: Mains

Lamb Chops and and Sicilian Olive Gremolata. . . . . GF

Pork Chops with Madeira-Poached Pears . . . . GF

"Four in Four" Coq au Vin. . . . . GF*

Pasta à la Sookie. . . . . V*

Chicken and Dumpling Casserole

Butternut Squash Pasta Purses V

Bracebridge Dinner Peacock Pie

Braised Lamb and Risotto . . . . GF*

Steak Haché with Peppercorn Sauce. . . . . GF*

Baron of Beef with Sauce Diane. . . . .GF*

Chapter Six: Drinks, Cocktails & Mixes

Wassai. . . . . V, V+, GF*

"Enscotched" Cocktail . . . . V, V+, GF*

Four Years without a Cocktail Mockaritas . . . . V, V+, GF

Stars Hollow Party Punch. . . . . V, V+, GF

Ginger Fizz . . . . V, V+, GF

Bacon-Infused Vodka Bloody Mary . . GF*

"Coffee! Coffee! Coffee!" Martini . . . V, GF*

Chocolate Chocolate Chip Milkshake . . V, GF*

Homemade Eggnog. . . . . V, GF

Ennui / Off-oui, "Oh, Hey, I'm Cured" Cocktail. . . . . V, V+, GF*

Chapter Seven: Desserts

Plum Pudding with Hard Sauce V

Raspberry Mousse with Candied Kumquats and Kumquat Gelée . . . . . GF

Sour Cream Peach Pie . . . . .V, GF*

"Paint the Wall Red" Strawberry Tarts . . . . V*

Rocky Road Cookies. . . . . V*

French Fantasy Crème Brûlée . . . . . . V, GF

Stars Hollow Says Goodbye Blackberry Pie. V

Muffin Bottom Meringue and Ice-Cream Pie. V

Chocolate Amaretto Mousse Cake (In the Shape of a G). . . . . V, GF

Cider Ice Cream . . . . V, GF

Zabaglione with Berries and Pine Nut Meringue Cookies. . . . . V, GF*

Dark Chocolate S'mores Wedding Cake

Check out my notes and tips on the recipes for ways to easily make a dish vegan, vegetarian, or gluten free.

Measurement Conversions

Kitchen Measurements

CUP	TABLESPOON	TEASPOON	FLUID OUNCES
1/16 cup	1 tablespoon	3 teaspoons	½ fluid ounce
⅛ cup	2 tablespoons	6 teaspoons	1 fluid ounce
¼ cup	4 tablespoons	12 teaspoons	2 fluid ounces
⅓ cup	5⅓ tablespoons	16 teaspoons	2⅔ fluid ounces
½ cup	8 tablespoons	24 teaspoons	4 fluid ounces
⅔ cup	10⅔ tablespoons	32 teaspoons	5⅓ fluid ounces
¾ cup	12 tablespoons	36 teaspoons	6 fluid ounces
1 cup	16 tablespoons	48 teaspoons	8 fluid ounces

GALLON	QUART	PINT	CUP	FLUID OUNCES
1/16 gallon	¼ quart	½ pint	1 cup	8 fluid ounces
⅛ gallon	½ quart	1 pint	2 cups	16 fluid ounces
¼ gallon	1 quart	2 pints	4 cups	32 fluid ounces
½ gallon	2 quarts	4 pints	8 cups	64 fluid ounces
1 gallon	4 quarts	8 pints	16 cups	128 fluid ounces

Oven Temperatures

CELCIUS	FAHRENHEIT
93°C	200°F
107°C	225°F
121°C	250°F
135°C	275°F
149°C	300°F
163°C	325°F
177°C	350°F
191°C	375°F
204°C	400°F
218°C	425°F
232°C	450°F

Weight

GRAMS	OUNCES
14 grams	½ ounce
28 grams	1 ounce
57 grams	2 ounces
85 grams	3 ounces
113 grams	4 ounces
142 grams	5 ounces
170 grams	6 ounces
283 grams	10 ounces
397 grams	14 ounces
454 grams	16 ounces
907 grams	32 ounces

Length

IMPERIAL	METRIC
1 inch	2.5 centimeters
2 inches	5 centimeters
4 inches	10 centimeters
6 inches	15 centimeters
8 inches	20 centimeters
10 inches	25 centimeters
12 inches	30 centimeters

About the Authors

ELENA P. CRAIG is a food and prop stylist and recipe developer with more than twenty-five years of experience in culinary design, marketing, photography, and publishing. With a deep love for pop culture, she enjoys hiding Easter eggs in depictions of fictional worlds. With her husband and two children, she has developed superhero cooking skills that cross generations, genders, and genres.

ELIZABETH FISH is a recipe developer and caterer with more than forty-five years in the food industry. She has lived in London, Istanbul, and New York City, and her love for food has gained her a community wherever she goes. Her interest in developing recipes started as a food columnist and cooking instructor for expats, teaching them how to make foods they were familiar with but using locally available ingredients. Her large extended family includes two children who share her love for food adventures and pickleball.

MICOL OSTOW is obsessed with pop culture. She's written dozens of books based on entertainment's biggest franchises, including *Roman Holiday: The Illustrated Storybook* and *Life Is Better with Friends*. She lives in New York with her family.

INSIGHT
EDITIONS
PO Box 3088
San Rafael, CA 94912
www.insighteditions.com

Find us on Facebook: www.facebook.com/InsightEditions
Follow us on Instagram: @insighteditions

ISBN: 979-8-88663-747-2

Publisher: Raoul Goff
SVP, Group Publisher: Vanessa Lopez
VP, Creative: Chrissy Kwasnik
VP, Manufacturing: Alix Nicholaeff
Editorial Director: Thom O'Hearn
Art Director: Stuart Smith
Senior Designer: Judy Wiatrek Trum
Senior Editor: Anna Wostenberg
Editorial Assistant: Sami Alvarado
VP, Senior Executive Project Editor: Vicki Jaeger
Production Manager: Deena Hashem
Strategic Production Planner: Lina s Palma-Temena

Recipes by Elena P. Craig and Elizabeth Fish
Written by Micol Ostow
Photography by Ted Thomas
Prop and food styling by Elena P. Craig
Food styling assistance by Patricia Parrish and Lauren Tedeschi

ROOTS of PEACE REPLANTED PAPER
Insight Editions, in association with Roots of Peace, will plant two trees for each tree used in the manufacturing of this book. Roots of Peace is an internationally renowned humanitarian organization dedicated to eradicating land mines worldwide and converting war-torn lands into productive farms and wildlife habitats. Roots of Peace will plant two million fruit and nut trees in Afghanistan and provide farmers there with the skills and support necessary for sustainable land use.

Manufactured in China by Insight Editions

10 9 8 7 6 5